AF379803

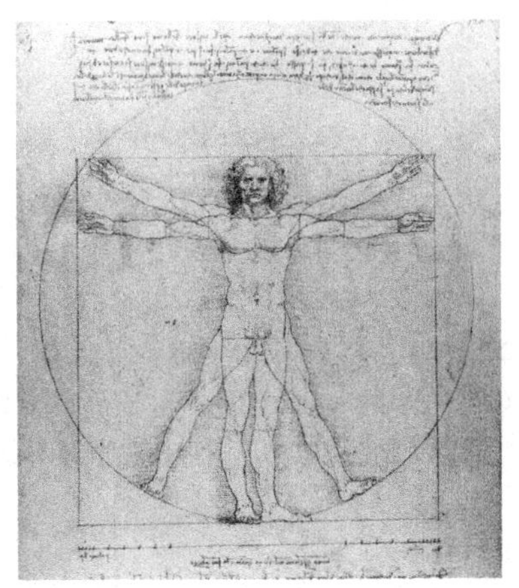

UNIVERSAL MAN
Da' Vinci's Soul Reborn

By RICHARD ALIBERTI

A concise and descriptive historical biography, into the life
and times of Leonardo da' Vinci, told from a modern day
perspective.

Salem House Press
PO Box 249
Salem MA 01970

ISBN-10: 0983666547
ISBN-13: 978-0-9836665-4-7
Library of Congress Number: 2012903801
First Edition 2019

,

When once you have tasted flight, you will forever walk the
earth with your eyes turned skyward, for there you have been,
and there you will always long to return.
~Leonardo da' Vinci

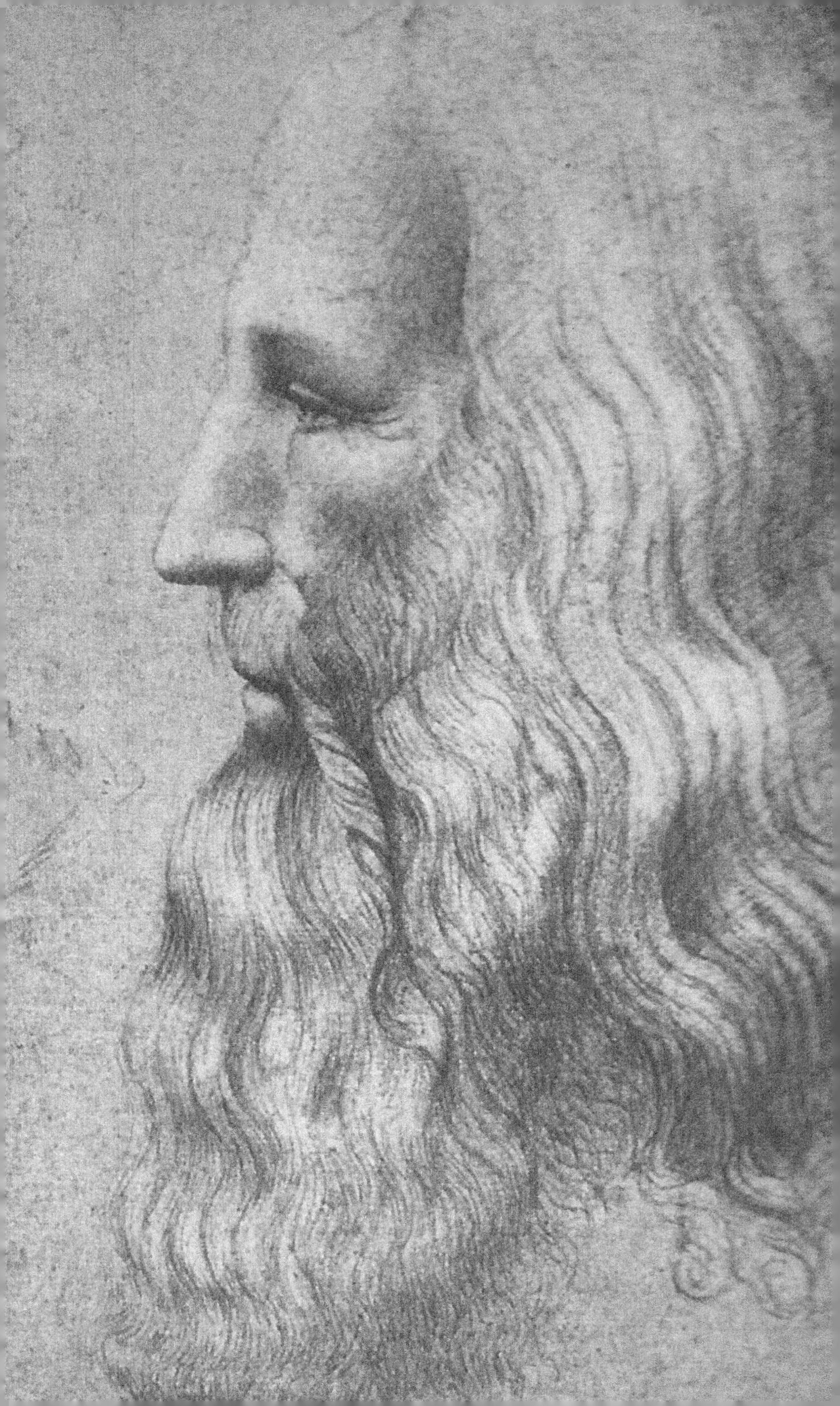

CHAPTERS

FOREWORD

In the normal course of events many men and women are born with various remarkable qualities and talents; but occasionally, in a way that transcends nature, a single person is marvelously, endowed by heaven with beauty, grace, and talent in such abundance that he leaves other men far behind, all his actions seem inspired, and indeed everything he does clearly comes from God rather from human art. Everyone acknowledged that this was true of Leonardo Da Vinci, an artist of outstanding physical beauty who displayed infinite grace in everything he did and who cultivated his genius so brilliantly that all problems he studied he solved with ease. He possessed great strength and dexterity; he was a man of regal spirit and tremendous breadth of mind; and his name became so famous that not only was he esteemed during his lifetime but his reputation endured and became even greater after his death.

Giorgio Vasari ~ around 1600

PREFACE

I believe we all share common traits as creative people. There is also a similarity of intuitive awareness and acute perception, coupled with an overall appreciation and value of beauty and truth. As I reverted back to all of the reading and research on the subject of Leonardo da' Vinci and the Renaissance artists, I began to identify with some of their experiences,and draw real strength from their bold and courageous nature and the period in which they flourished. Because of this simple fact, I was enabled to move forward, often without any fear or trepidation with regards to the commitment and dedication required when engaged in the creative process.

As a child, I was brought up in a very warm and loving environment. There were seven children in my family, and my father was a builder and a teacher, born into a family of Italian immigrant builders. My grandmother was an artists and a musician. There was a continuous and powerful bond of love and faith with this family. My great grandmother lived to be 104 years old and possessed a beautiful soul as did my grandmother and her sisters. They were the most beautiful loving beings one could possibly imagine. The kindness and care I received was naturally conducive to my spiritual growth as a very young boy. This later became an important reason for me to identify with Leonardo and to experience what I found to be an apparent symbiotic and hereditary potentiality that is inherent in our separate beings; In simpler terms, like family or blood relatives.

As I read more about Leonardo's childhood, I found real identification and so I decided to expand my reading and writing out of curiosity and began to piece together some of these aspects. As I delved deeper into this extraordinary human being and rich period in art history, I became captivated by the pure creative energy present during his times. What on earth, I began to think to myself, could be more beautiful to an artist, than to grow up in a climate of such creative splendor? A civilization of promise, born out of a true cultural spirit! I can only imagine such a reality and surmise to such circumstances in earnest.

For nearly two years each night, I found myself leaving my world and my work behind for the vicarious and continuous pleasures of a fourteenth and fifteenth century blissful sojourn. It became apparent that what I had started as a short thesis demanded much more attention than I initially anticipated.

I began to reflect on my first years at the Museum School in Boston and remember some very fine days filled with beautiful moments of joy as I first entered the halls of that school. The studios were filled with enthusiasm; there were creative objects strewn about. Drawings and paintings on the walls, clay and plaster sculptures being worked on, the scent of raw linseed oil and graphite permeated my senses and the excitement of the students all there for the same reasons, to create and to feel a spark of creativity and express their joy for life.

I could cross the street to the Museum of Fine Arts, enter its massive Roman Revival entrance way with its giant colonnade, see the great statues of antiquity, touch them with my hands and relish in their beauty. I became a part of it all. This is what I wanted, to work in a purely inspirational and creative world; to make objects and pictures of beauty at every possible turn.

Perhaps this is another important similarity I share with Leonardo. Attending art school, I could identify with Leonardo, as when he first encountered the great city of Florence and its magnificent beauty. His invitation into the studio of his great master, Verrocchio, and all the students there to welcome him into their fascinating world. Of course, one could hardly compare Florence, Italy to Boston, Massachusetts, however the personal feelings must have been similar. During those early years at the Museum School as an art student, I would learn the rudiments of painting, drawing, sculpture, and begin to explore the possibilities involved in these time tested trades.

I would imagine how my fifteenth century heroes would go about their introduction into this extraordinary realm of activity and inspiration. Trying hard not to forget the most important values Leonardo and his contemporaries had instilled in me and the creative spirit I discovered in them as I began writing this book and experimenting with new processes of discovery, I inadvertently found even more inspiration. As I began to peel away some of the layers of what seemed to be a massive and formidable undertaking, I found scores of towering geniuses thriving during the Italian Renaissance, some of which being the teachers, friends, and associates of Leonardo.

I also found a rich history of no less than three hundred years of near inconceivable artistic achievement and human cultural development. Under these layers I rediscovered Leonardo da' Vinci, not as the old white-bearded crazy wizard that some of the lesser are inclined to think of him as, but as a man of flesh and blood and tremendous virtue. A man who lived, worked, and died for the betterment and advancement of Humankind; a man that possessed a beautiful heart, a beautiful soul, and a beautiful mind.

I wanted to express the importance I found in this fact, in relation to myself, showing him in an equal yet different light. Using what I have learned as an artist and to convey as clearly and concisely as possible some of the more important qualities we have as artists.

In 1984 I left the Museum School and was living in an old factory building in Boston's South End. The building was a long brick structure and the street was of cobble stone. There were many artists, craftsmen, and musicians living in this building and the surrounding area. There were great studio spaces with large windows and high ceilings. The south end of Boston was the place for artists, along with parts of Chinatown and the Fort Point area, which was across the channel into South Boston.

Thayer Street was special in that it housed many of us, a concentration of non-stop creativity and music under one large roof. This is when I began to combine my sculpture with music and experiment with every medium I could find. Initially I worked with clay as I did at the Museum School, with live models and learned the methods of bronze casting and welding at the nearby Mass College of Art Foundry. Thayer Street was one of many abandoned mill buildings that became a bastion of artists living in this post-industrial gritty area of Boston. The elevated highway and trains were a stone's throw away. Directly across the street from my door was, and still stands, an old structure styled after the medieval Siennse towers of the 12th century Italian lookouts. It was a source of inspiration. I was living a day-to-day existence with many new friends and fellow artists that would generously share their time and ideas on many occasions. There was a good vibe in the air in those early days in Boston.

I began collecting large quantities of material to assemble into sculpture such as discarded aluminum and steel, large pieces of Styrofoam and plastic, forms taken from construction sites. I was spray-painting and creating installations and simultaneously working with kinetic sculptures and performing music.

The sculptures were crude and industrial, made mostly of found objects; cast aluminum and linear forms that were powered by motors. The music was experimental, rooted in industrial, electronic and ambient influences. With a percussionist, I performed all over Boston and Cambridge and was invited to perform at the Museum School in a well-known art space called Mobius.

It was during this period I had the opportunity to meet one of my musical influences, Brian Eno, who performed and spoke at the Museum School in 1988. I left the Museum School and moved into a large space on the edge of Chinatown. It was above an old abandoned strip club on LaGrange Street located in what was then called the Combat Zone, one of the very first red-light districts in the country. "The Zone", as we refer to it was notorious and seedy, but in decline at the time.

Several years after this period I had the opportunity to travel to the Middle East to explore some of the ruins of antiquity and then to Europe seeing Italy and France for the first time. This is where I first encountered the works of many great Renaissance masters and caught the spirit of Leonardo da' Vinci. This is where I truly felt his presence in a more profound and vital sense. For the first time in my life I could feel my origins and realize a kinship with the masters I studied at the Museum School, and begin to identify with their world.

When I returned to my work in Boston there was very little in the way of patronage and support for the fine artists in Boston. In 1992 I had the opportunity to live and work as a full time artist in the North End of Boston, in the Italian Quarter. I opened a small shop where I sold my bronze sculptures, began working in photography and designing and fabricating furniture. It was a beautiful space with frontage on Salem Street only two blocks from the Old North Church. I lived and worked in that shop, creating and living a dream for the better part of a decade. The space would later become a gallery and facilitate several commissions to create large-scale bronze sculptures and design various architectural and decorative elements for the local patronage.

I received commissions to create bronzes for several universities, the Dante Aligheri Society in Cambridge, and churches throughout Greater Boston. My smaller Bronze figurines were finding their way into many private collections. The North End, at this time, was predominantly still Italian and proved to be conducive to many of my creative efforts. I had some very wonderful years there and became known throughout the area for creating and providing inspiration through my art.

It was an advantageous time for me as well, when I began to realize my potential, and I could actually make a living with my talents. The Aliberti Gallery, as it was called, was at first another experiment. I began with no expectations at all, having experienced so much hardship in Boston for over 15 years. I had very little hope of making a living as an artist, however the North End, for me, was different. For every moment there, I flourished and enjoyed a small bit of success. Perhaps this is one of the relevant aspects that came to my realization, which I shared with Leonardo.

I looked back to those days and realized that I did affect change in that little quarter of Boston and perhaps even inspired some of the people and their children there. The gallery opened in the spring of 1992, and became a meeting place for many artists and writers from the Boston area. It was also frequented by patrons from all over the world. Many of them would express to me their feelings of the experience they encountered in the gallery. For a brief moment in time, they felt as though they had walked into a beautiful little bottega in Italy. It seemed my efforts allowed them to escape from the hustle and bustle of their busy days, if only for a brief moment.

I hope this book will provide you with the same effect.

ACKNOWLEDGEMENTS

To: my son Michael, my mother and father, Petra, and my dear friends Anthony Martignetti, and Rob Miniero, and Albert Gawet and the Gawet family for their gracious support.

INTRODUCTION

This book was written from an artist's perspective and from my own experience as a creative individual. What you are about to read is the culmination of seven years researching, and writing about the subject of Leonardo Da Vinci, his life and his times, and some thoughts on the realities and important moments that contributed to this extraordinary human being. He was a man of great talent and scope of mind, and to this day many believe him to be one of, if not, the most brilliant and influential figures to have ever lived.

In this condensed work you will discover some extraordinary facts about Leonardo Da Vinci, and you will also experience a certain degree of inspiration and encounter a new found appreciation for the wonderful artist/ scientist/engineer and philosopher he truly was. You will embark on a spiritual journey of the most fascinating kind, during what could be called the most creative and culturally advanced period in world history, known as the Italian Renaissance.

There have been very few artists that have written in length on the subject of Leonardo Da Vinci. Giorgio Vasari, who lived and worked in the fifteenth century as an artist, architect, and writer, wrote a work in three parts that included no less than two hundred of the many great artists of the Italian Renaissance. In his book Lives of the Artists, he wrote some very beautiful and poignant words about Leonardo, as he did with many of the artists included in his book; however, he did not write in length about Leonardo in particular. He was closer in age and more familiar with the work of his friends Michelangelo Buonarrotti and Raphael Sanzio de Urbino, to name but a few, hence he wrote more extensively about them. His perspective as artist and friend of many of the artists mentioned in his book has provided the world with some of the only historical documentation in existence.

Universal Man is not a book about the inner workings of Leonardo Da Vinci's mind, or what prompted him to work the way he did, nor is it a treatise on his paintings, or an in depth analysis on his psychology. This book is a personal exploration, and a concise historical biography, interspersed with some of my own feelings and thoughts including some colorful poetical interpretations. There are now in existence countless volumes written about this enigmatic genius, by many historians and scholars from all over the world, however it is rare to find anything written about him by an artist other than Giorgio Vasari.

Through my own exploration I found this genius entwined in an endless web of mystery and misinformation which compelled me to discover more about him. It's as if the layers upon layers of mysterious fact and fiction written about Leonardo da' Vinci over the centuries have intermingled for so long that it has enabled these facts to become distorted and more difficult to actually make real determinations as to how and why things were the way they were, and what actually did occur during his time. So

I offer my thoughts and observations with the keenest intuitive sense I can muster, as an artist and free-thinking individual, and with as much care and accuracy about my subject possible. To many of us Leonardo was superhuman in every sense of the word that had no equal. Even amongst his peers there were none that possessed such a rich and abundant diversity of mind and natural ability.

 As I continued to study this great figure, I began to draw from the sheer magnitude of his creative energy, his acuity and the multitude of gifts he possessed. I found myself often overwhelmed by the extraordinary complexities and knowledge he put forth with such ease, and the precision to execute his ideas with such depth and acute foresight. I was, and still am fascinated by this great genius. As I continued to discover more about Leonardo, I found myself becoming more perceptive in my own life and as a direct result of this I became more prolific in my pursuit as an artist.

 During the course of my research, Leonardo began to emerge as a man that breathed the same air as I, and I found my purpose, along with sufficient reason in that purpose, and even more importantly I found inspiration and truth. This in of itself has emboldened me to carry on as a creative individual. With these attributes I became somewhat fearless and open to many new areas of discovery. During this process of discovery, I became aware of the world around me like never before, and I began to incorporate some of these wonderful attributes that I have discovered while engaged in my own creative life.

 It is fair to say that most all people who encounter Leonardo either in spirit or material form are awestruck by his overwhelming genius. There are millions of artists who share adoration for his legacy, as well as scholars, historians and people who have a great passion for the arts. I believe that most of us can appreciate who he was, and what he did because of the beautiful spiritual presence, which still resides in his work and fascinates us all. This is one of if not the primary reasons I decided to write about him and his world, my identification of that spirit.

Leonardo Da Vinci's artwork has been copied, reproduced, and written about more than any other artwork in the entire history of art. To this day his fame continues to grow, and he still continues to inspire all of us.

Universal Man was written to enlighten, educate, and also serve as a guide as well as a chronological essay into the extraordinary circumstances that were present during Leonardo's lifetime. It will briefly describe many of his numerous, colorful and brilliant contemporaries and their significance.

During the Quattrocento, or 15th century, scores of many very interesting and eccentric personalities were present during Leonardo's lifetime. In this book I introduce some of the closest and most influential ones he encountered. There are also many creative individuals mentioned in this book that may seem inconsequential to the reader; however, I assure you that they are truly significant and great in their own right.

I have accumulated many facts regarding these artists that I believe to be credible. There is a sufficient amount of historical evidence in existence as well. Much of the source material available is limited but none-the-less accurate.

CHAPTER 1

THE BEGINNINGS OF INFLUENCE AND SPIRIT

THERE exist in this life many things that are not fully understood, esoteric things, like the origin of ideas and thoughts, our feelings and perceptions, our spirituality and the soul, things that we accept as part of our human nature without questioning them, things that are too immense and profound to ever fully grasp or comprehend, things that make this life so wonderful to live.

Leonardo da' Vinci was an extraordinarily fascinating human being who lived nearly six hundred years ago, and to this day still remains to be one of the most spiritually evocative and enigmatic souls to have ever graced the Earth. He somehow made his way into my mind, when I was only a child. I don't question how this happened; I only know that it did.

As in many sensitive and creative people all over this world, his spirit began to have a profound effect on me, and for a brief moment in time, I became captivated by this spirit and believed that I could be like him. It was not at all relevant that he was from a very distant and completely different period in time. It was his affect that was so profound and fascinating to me. What could be more satisfying, I thought to myself, to be special like Leonardo da' Vinci, to be creative as an artist, working within a beautiful realm of ideas and dreams, and to realize such a lofty pursuit of a creative life.

I didn't think about much more at the time, however I really believed that I found my calling.

I was around seven or eight years old, and it was later in life during my teenage years when I learned of Leonardo's true greatness. Of course, I still wanted to emulate him. To me, he made art a very serious and rational occupation to pursue, and he represented such wonderful and promising ideals. He was the only figure in history that I really cared for. I came to the realization that it was his illuminating spirit that I came into contact with and it's profound effect has stayed with me ever since.

In my early twenties, I remember someone once saying to me that I was a dreamer. I thought for a moment about it, and I remembered that I liked the way that sounded. I thought, weren't all great men dreamers? Wasn't Leonardo a dreamer? I wanted to believe that I had something Leonardo had and I wanted to realize my potential as an artist and as a creative individual.

Today I believe more than ever in dreams because I have realized some of them, and heretofore I believe there have been no persons more influential in my life than Leonardo da' Vinci, besides my parents who brought me into this world. This great courageous figure and his legacy has made way for most all creative people throughout the world. He has enabled us to see with new eyes, the inner workings of nature and the beauty it embodies. He has shown and taught us incredible and timeless things, such as how to look at life in a fuller, more meaningful way, and how to live in a more meaningful way as well. All of this had a profound influence on the world and has contributed to my own synthesis as an artist and experimenter.

It was his brilliant light and gift to show the world the vitality of a truly creative soul, and the possibility of achieving the highest degree of perfection attainable. Leonardo has demonstrated to me triumph of will, longevity, and truth. He has enabled me to understand true discipline, through patience and endurance.

These are just several of the many important qualities I have gained from studying him. They are the gifts in life itself and the love for the knowledge he has so gracefully bequeathed to the world. They are the sensory gifts we enjoy, such as our very own talents to perceive things as they are and appear to be, and our capacity to behold the Divine, which is what the arts truly celebrate, and Leonardo has exemplified this on many different levels.

There exist other things in this life that we experience, temporal in nature, that reside in the physical world that we all share and we experience together collectively; things like aesthetics or beauty. Like most of us, I work towards Ideals and into systems of my choosing, and together we can and usually do experience a collective understanding in these systems.

We share values like beauty. Beauty is a thing, I believe, Leonardo valued very highly, and so do most people. It is our choice and we value it very highly. What we feel to be beautiful in this world for instance is quite remarkable for example; most of us believe that Tuscany is a beautiful place, and that Vivaldi composed some very beautiful violin concertos, and that a great piece of music or art is great for sufficient reasons. It satisfies certain criteria among other things, and it makes us feel pleasure.

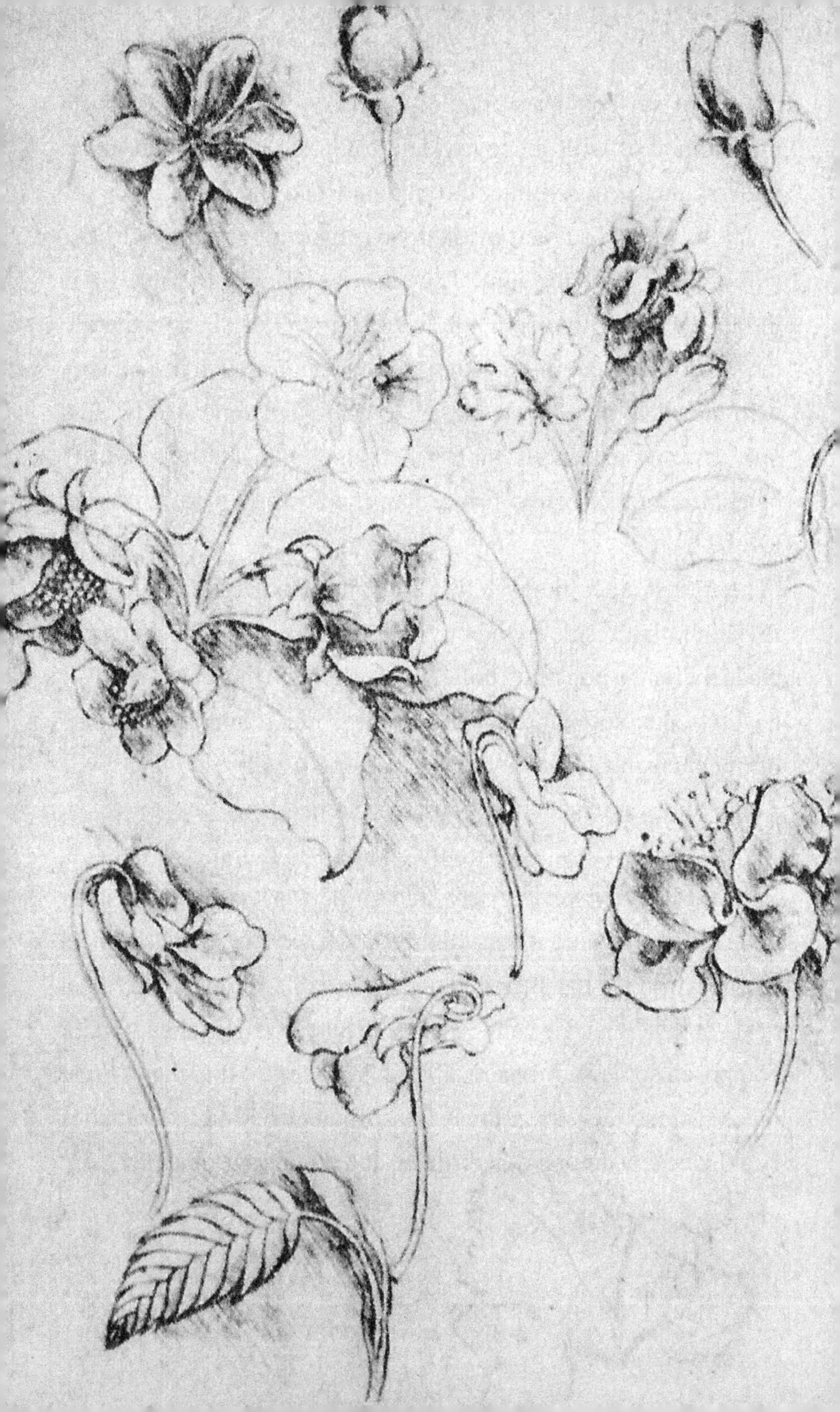

Collective reasoning is a part of our collective consciousness. To me there is no avoiding this, whether it's a beautiful woman, a mountainous vista, or a splendid piece of art, it could be the smell of orange blossoms, the taste of honey, or a bakery baking fresh bread. We are always drawn to beauty; most of us prefer beauty instead of ugliness. These are things in which we still adhere to as a culture. We desire them and aspire towards them. They are ideas and values going back to the beginnings of civilization in Mesopotamia, Egypt, Greece and Rome ,and later the Italian Renaissance, which was a direct result of such ideals and principles like aesthetics.

Let us Begin our Voyage on this Beautiful Peninsula.

Sometime around 50 BC, in and around Rome, there lived a great philosopher, statesman, and lawyer by the name of Marcus Tillius Cicero who introduced the Romans to the chief schools of Greek philosophy and created part of the Latin vocabulary. He created words like humanitas that asserted man's importance as a cultivated being and in control of his moral universe, and Virtue, another beautiful word and idea meaning nature perfected and developed to its highest degree. In that realm exists a resemblance between man and God.

Cicero, who lived more than fifteen hundred years before the Italian Renaissance, was one of the most important proponents of its existence. His works rank amongst some of the most vital and influential achievements in European culture. His extant writings and philosophy encouraged and inspired the great men and woman of the Renaissance enormously. There were of course many of whom contributed to his advancement as well, his predecessors Plato and Aristotle, Socrates and Parmenides to name but a few.

All of these giants would contribute immeasurably to Cicero's vision and the rebirth of Greco-Roman ideals and principles. They gave way to a true Renaissance that included art, literature, and science as a viable and tangible way to interpret life and human behavior. As a matter of fact, most of these ideas and principles still shape the way we think and live today.

Many of us are unaware that Marcus Cicero, a man that lived nearly two thousand years ago, deeply inspired the Founding Fathers of the United States of America, and the revolutionaries of France. John Adams, considered to be the most ethical of all the founding fathers, held Cicero in high esteem and gave prudence to Cicero's great statesmanship. Thomas Jefferson studied Cicero throughout most of his life and believed him to be the most eloquent philosopher in history. But, it was around six hundred years ago when his philosophical principles and profound ideas manifest themselves into a movement of epic proportions becoming known as the early Renaissance.

Cicero's writings are considered to be the most influential works in European culture, and responsible for all of the important western humanist principles we share today. They first began to emerge in Italy where they would take hold and become inherent among such diamond minds as Dante Alighieri, Albertino Mussato, Francesco Petrarca, Giovanni Boccaccio, Leonardo Bruni and Leon Aliberti to name but a few, and immediately after in the plastic arts, Giotto di Bondone, Tomasso Massacio, Lorenzo Ghiberti, and Donato Donatello. With these masters along with scores of other great thinkers came a bold unprecedented new age in culture and with it a dynamic and masterful period of virtue and aesthetic achievement.

THE very beginnings of the Renaissance took place during the mid to late thirteen hundreds and ended around sixteen hundred. It was considered the first progressive movement in that it would bring us out of antiquity and the middle ages and into a new era of awareness. Towards the beginning of the fourteenth century there lived the great scholar and poet laureate Francesco Petrarca (Petrarch), His name at birth was actually Francesco Pertacco, known as the father of humanism and precursor to the Renaissance, he would usher in a new age of human triumph and distinguish the dark ages from the early years of this new period in which he became a prime mover. With an exquisite mind and illuminating verse he became a celebrity throughout Europe and his sonnets were broadly admired and imitated as well. He traveled throughout Europe served as an ambassador and became one of the first poet laureates since antiquity.

He was a prolific writer and became a model for lyrical poetry, as a proponent of Cicero he was highly instrumental in the recovery of the ancient Latin writings of antiquity as well. Petrarch has been credited for creating the concept of the Dark Ages. A close friend of Petrarch was Giovanni Boccaccio, another genius known for poetic brilliance and unprecedented verisimilitude, His work exemplifies some of the most beautiful verse in the history of poetry. Boccaccio's *Decameron* was and still remains a masterpiece among the world's greatest literature.

Several years later a man by the name of Leonardo Bruni would follow in their footsteps. He was another brilliant humanist historian and secularist who would translate the works of Plato and Aristotle and write a biography on Cicero and a history book on the Florentine people. That work incidentally is considered the first book ever to be written on history. He developed a three period view of history -- Antiquity, the Middle Ages, and the first modern age known as the Renaissance. It was Bruni who penned the phrase studia humanitas, the study of human endeavors which draws a distinction from theology and metaphysics.

Try for a moment to imagine these fine fellows in their colorful robes and fine fabric headdress walking along soft earthen pathways beneath warm magenta evening skies that gently lay over stone houses with terra-cotta roofs and carved wooden doors, the stairs rustic, timeworn, fixed to stucco walls of faded soft yellow pigment nestled between tall medieval towers and smoothly carved ancient Roman columns, lovely piazzas, serene and still, sit timelessly between broken statues, spiritual, evocative and beautiful; green exotic cypress trees line the dirt roads and dot the hilly landscape. Children, shoe less and happy, laugh and run around archaic ruins, several goats, pigs, dogs and chickens wonder freely, as the warm air flows over the landscape, soft melodic sounds of a lute and the beautiful voice of a peasant girl singing poetic Italian verse. In the distance the soft clang of church bells, punctuate this serene ambiance, Tuscany is strewn with love and promise.

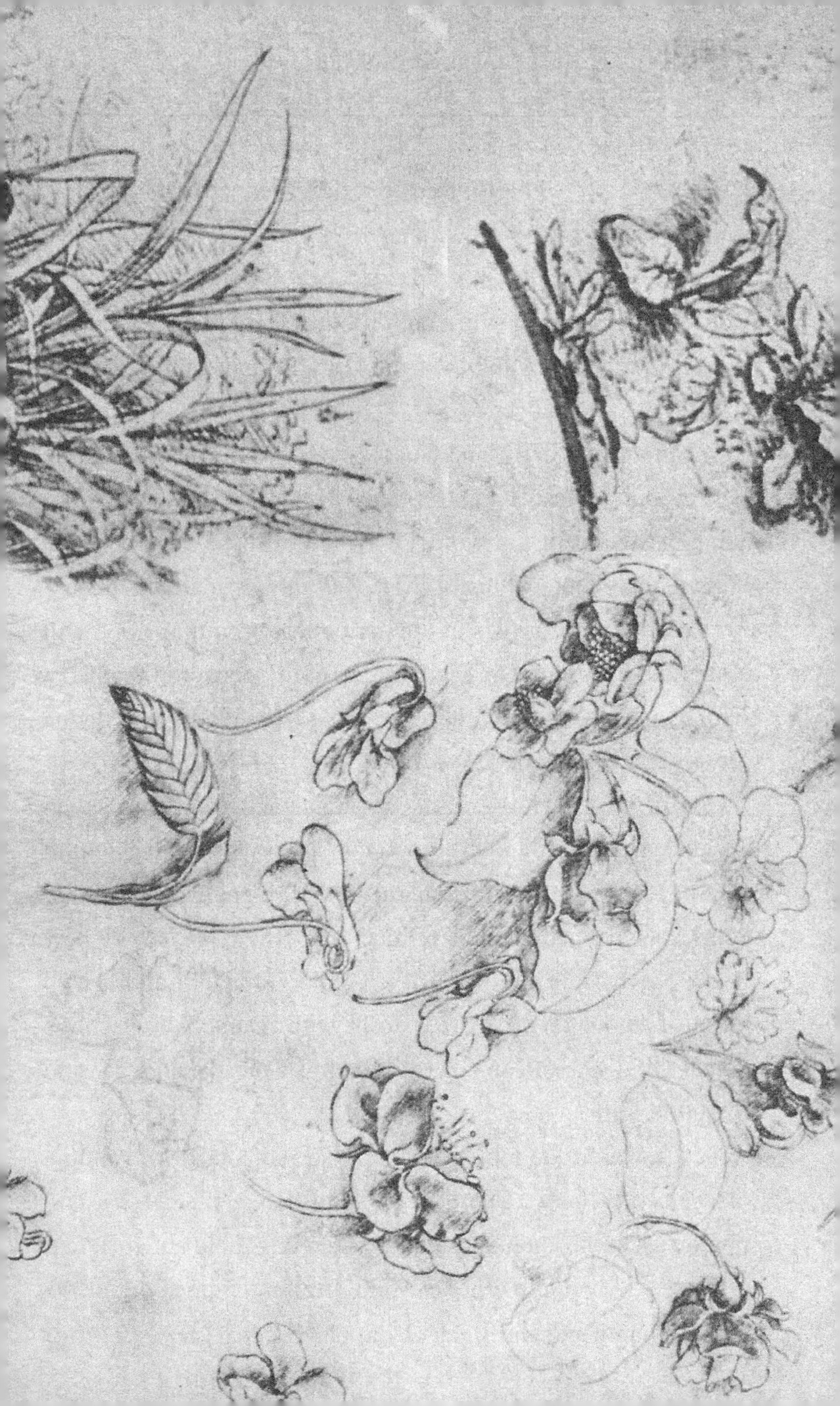

The Birth of Poetic Verse

At the beginning of the thirteenth century there lived a great and powerful king who ruled over the Holy Roman Empire. It was 1220.

He came from Sicily, and was a man of extraordinary culture, energy, and ability. King Frederic II known as the "stupor mundi" (wonder of the world) was one of those very rare and brilliant great Kings of history. He was a lover of art and poetry, a true patron to the artists of the period that promoted good will throughout his reign. His Sicilian school of poets promulgated a courageous new age of culture, which was begun by his Magna Curia (great court) poets.

One of these leading poets was Giacomo da' Lentini who invented the sonnet and Guittone d'Arezzo who contributed to early poetic structure. Not long after the Magna Curia, another group was formed named (Dolce Stil Novo) "a sweet new style", born from the likes of a Guido Guinizelli and a well spring of romantic verse spew forth with Dante Alighieri, his friends Guido Cavalcanti, Lapo Gianni, Cino da' Pistoia, and Brunetto Latini.

They nurtured the rebirth in its artistic infancy with sublime verse and ingenuity. They went on to create new styles and approaches to the languages they mastered. A bold and different reality would begin to emerge as civilization climbed out of the dark ages and into the light of the early Renaissance. Try for a moment to imagine, how these poetic minds would interpret their world and their thoughts and feelings towards the distant past, while still aware of the purity and innocence of the times at hand. To them, being engaged with anything else in the world other than the beautiful, rich Tuscan world and it's environs in which they stood, working their craft, writing and reciting would not seem rational.

The significance it held and the new age of a creative culture that they would foster became imminent. Along with Italy's proud past, a great and far reaching Roman Empire lay buried beneath its sacred ground. For this was the sacred land of the old Roman Kings and Republic, recognized and remembered. Underneath these roads and fields of Italy lie the great Roman era, with its five hundred year existence so long and lost but barely forgotten. Left behind were the great legends and myths, the art, artifice, and a great Empires demise. This magnificent age of unimaginable glory lingered above the ruins of Italy only in spirit amongst the remaining crumbled art and architecture that lay dormant until the artists and writers of the Renaissance exhumed it.

The Renaissance became inevitable and unstoppable well after a thousand years of fire and fragmentation. These men of the early Renaissance understood their roles as arbiters of truth, love, and beauty. They would begin by synthesizing their true Roman spirit with their Etruscan boldness and become extraordinarily courageous individuals.

Imagine life in fourteenth century Italy; rustic and crude with all the natural world of Tuscany and its majestic splendor still in control. There had to have been some very sweet and precious moments for many of the Italian people living in this historic and beautiful setting in its capital, Florence, and its countryside.

The different climates of Italy are significant in many ways, a contributing factor, unique and varied providing a wide variety of fruits and vegetation and the surrounding Mediterranean Sea with its abundant fishing ports of commerce and trade. The Italian peninsula, we should remember, was very isolated compared to the landlocked countries of Europe, and its ports provided entrance of unprecedented wealth and patronage from all over the known world. The massive natural barrier created by the Alps in the northern regions was no doubt a contributing factor as well.

These aspects may very well have been reason for the extraordinary amount of creative and intellectual activity on the peninsula. Moreover the amalgamation of ethnicity and bloodlines for centuries intermixed, should not be overlooked. If we were to trace some of this DNA I have no doubt it would prove to be a most perfect example. Initially made up of Greco-Roman bloodlines infused with the Etruscan sea fairing tribes that inhabited the seven hills of Rome, and later, although no one can be sure to the time lines of an influx of Arabic influences that infiltrated the south, and later still the northern Germanic tribes as well. All together a most extraordinary gene pool the likes of none other in the history of the world.

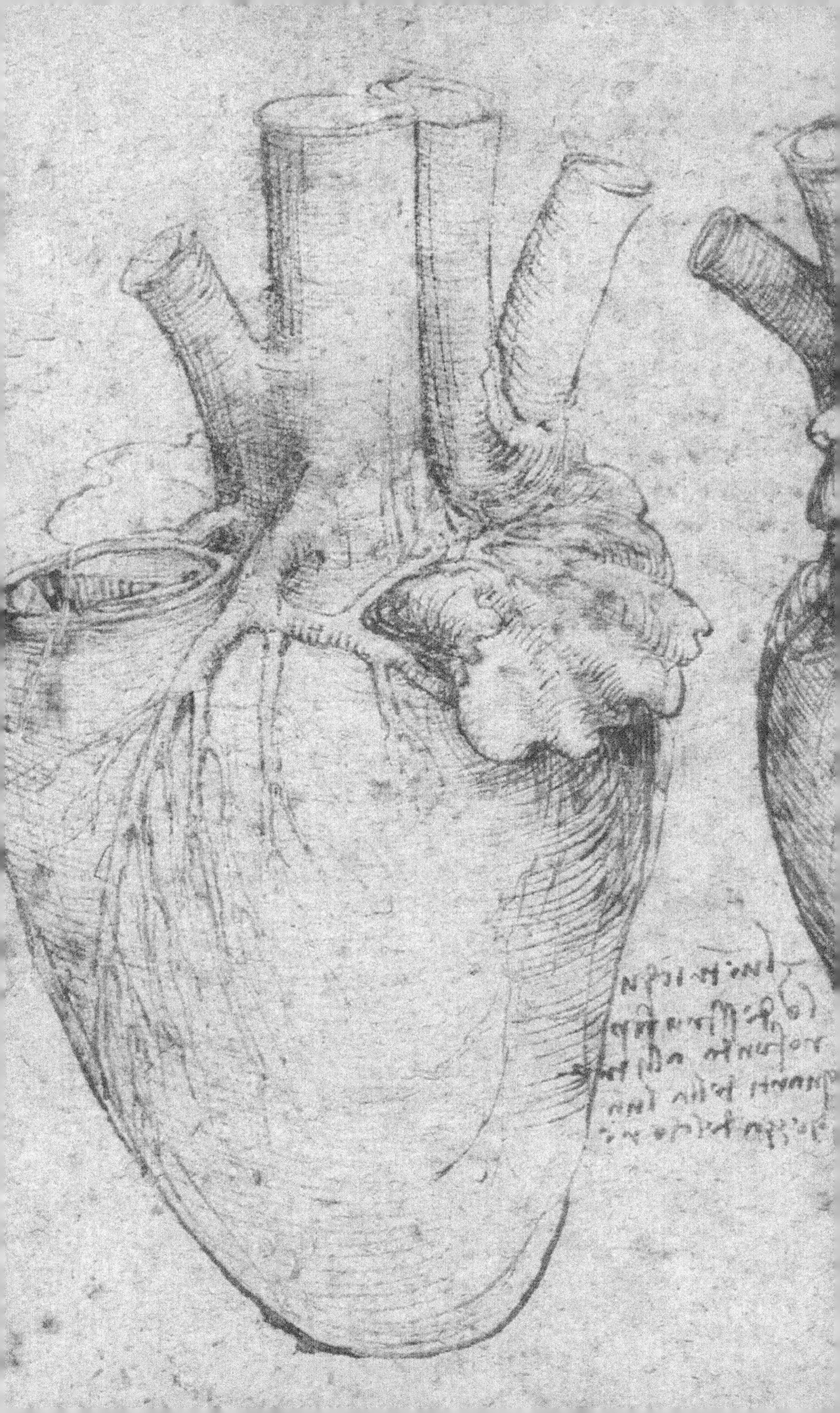

CHAPTER 3

A JUXTAPOSITION OF TWO REALITIES

TO try and understand the realities and comprehend the thinking processes of the Renaissance mind is quite fascinating. In many respects I believe that we as twenty first century people share very few similarities with the aesthetes of the fourteenth and fifteenth centuries. The conditions were far more conducive to a life for them to flourish. I also believe that many of these men and women were very pure in ways that are too distant to describe with any real accuracy.

The poet/ artist mind of the Renaissance was different in their capacity to think freely and creatively, inventing spontaneously while concentrating their efforts without many distractions, and many of them exercising their energies on several disciplines simultaneously. This distinction is quite extraordinary in itself. The way in which they perceived their world was quite different as well. Time moved at a much slower pace and life was simplified by the innocence of the age. I don't believe they were as vain or nearly as self-conscious as we are today. And their focus as broad and distracted as ours is.

We will never know how they actually perceived their world but I am sure it was with a much less obstructed consciousness. There presently exists an overabundant amount of external stimulus that we as twenty first century people are exposed to daily, and the element of time it seems has sped up and has become extremely invasive to many of us. Like many millions of young American children living in a vast suburban sprawl.

We are first exposed to various assorted stimuli at a tender young age. For many of us there was Dr. Suess, Walt Disney, Hanna and Barbera, and the Looney Tunes. Bugs Bunny was a favorite amongst all the crazy wonderful characters of animation that were transmitted into our homes and brains daily. Then there were the storybooks, the newspapers and magazines, the telephones, the radios, and the records we played and movies we went to see. In my teenage years there were only three major networks and channel 2 to deal with. Everyone seemed to have been on the same page as far as the available media and state of the art technology was concerned, however the external stimuli was in full swing.

Another interesting aspect was that we were always reminded of the" time" as youngsters, whether it was time for school or time for dinner. Time was always intruding or lingering in the subconscious. With the advent of cable networks the PC, the internet, video games, later the laptop, the smart phone and the MP3, things became overwhelming to a large degree yet fascinating and at the same time became essential to many of us.

This electronic blitz I refer to by the way has occurred only in the past thirty five years! It has contributed significantly to the most profound change in human behavior since our beginnings. One could look at these facts objectively with complete disdain and even sadness after one realizes how superficially limited and controlled much of this stimuli is, and was to be subjected to, for decades as a youth. The vast majority of us did not grow up in beautiful historic ruins, or in bucolic surroundings observing beautiful frescos and sculptures daily, nor reading Dante, Petrarch or Boccaccio. We were and continue to be consumed by instantaneous gratification via disposable ephemera and electronic media while being force fed consumerism.

I wanted to illustrate this contrasting imagery concerning time so as to provide an understanding to the overall conditioning that may have helped facilitate the extraordinary amount of intellectual fertility present in Italy during the Renaissance. This aide in describing some of the reasoning I feel that has stifled our thought processes in so many ways. In some respects it has nearly annihilated our overall capacity to think creatively and to live as a creative culture.

Since my adulthood I have always been very cautious in my dealings with high technology. I believe the computer and the internet are good tools if used properly, and used when necessary. The television had immense potential in so many ways yet tragically became a tool for consumerism and stupidity. We find that high technology has a tendency to be somewhat isolating and to a good degree divisive and exclusionary, however we do enjoy the speed of it.

There now exists an electronic barrier between the artist and the finite instruments of creativity. That being said there are now very fascinating and gifted individuals using these technologies for art and music, and there is some very interesting art being made. Some working in the film and video game industry have had their moments with the use of the new technologies to a large degree, and music has made some significant breakthroughs.

However there are not many creative film makers and musicians using these technologies, and most of the films and video games now being created are geared towards infantile animation fantasies, sports, gore, and war. As far as the plastic arts (sculpture/ painting) are concerned, most people have very limited access to them as well. We may find an image on the internet or even glance at a magazine, however most of us do not experience art first hand. Sadly, the majority never pays a visit to an art museum, and much of the artwork still being pushed on the public is either from the 1800's French impressionists period, or from the early 20th century and up to the 1960's. If one studies the artwork generated during the 1960's for example as I have, a good majority of it for the most part is very poor aesthetically.

In simpler terms, it is ugly!

That's not to say that there have not been good ideas, and concepts generated during this past half century and some great advances in video and installation work. There has been some very stimulating conceptual art work created as well. Perhaps more adequate creativity and beauty will return in the plastic arts in the coming years, and become more accessible to the masses through various applications of computer technology, but only if the newer generations embrace these so called technological advances with more attention towards aesthetics will it occur.

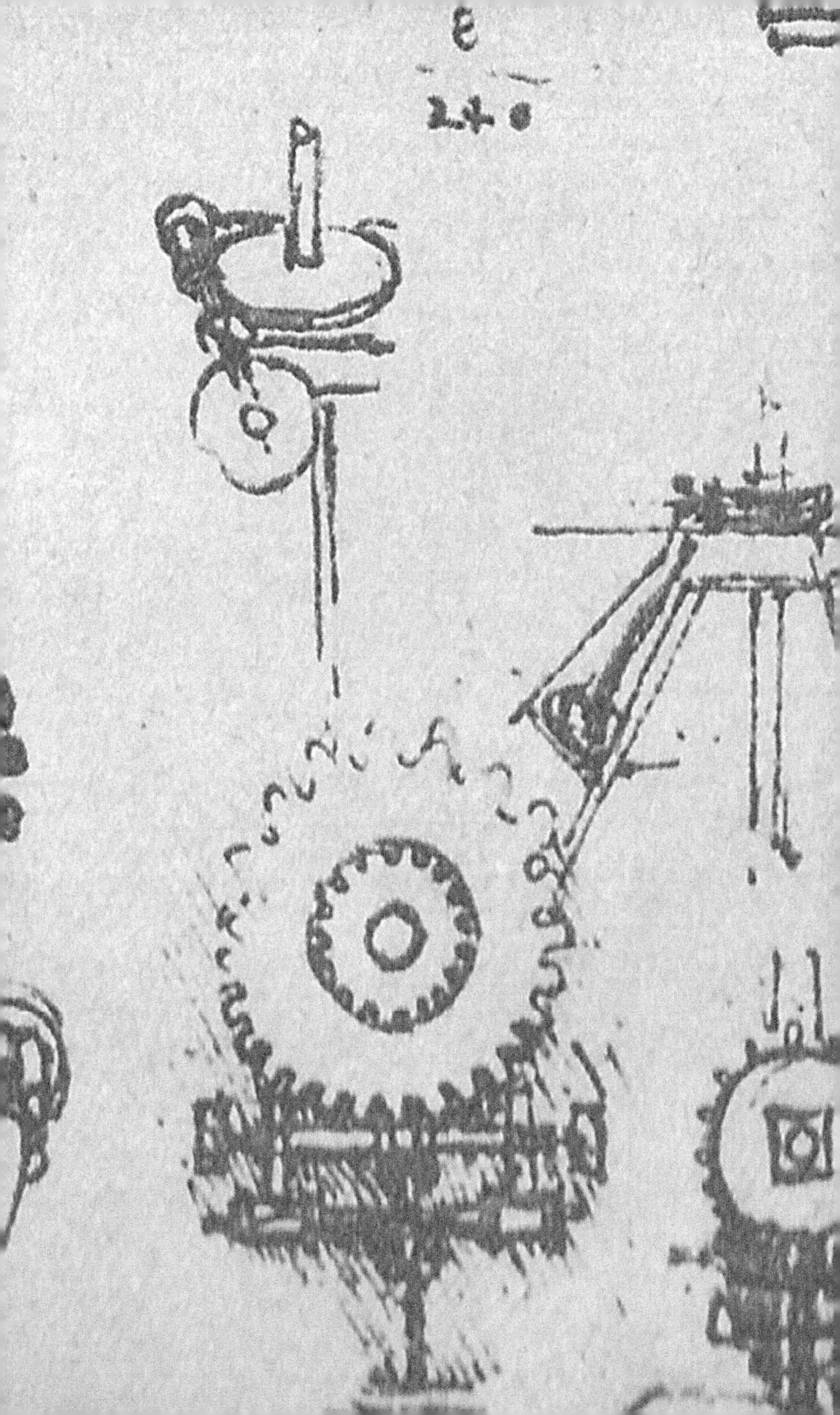

~CHAPTER 4~
THE PLACE AND THE TIME
- The proof is in the Peninsula

TRY for a moment to think of this place in time when innocence prevailed and the rest of the world was perceived as a vast and mysterious enigma. We can find complete solace in our own contemporary realm of thought through our imaginations and recall the verses of a beautiful poem by Dante or Francesco Petrarca, and then picture in our minds the realities of the times, and experience the joy they encountered as creative individuals. We can see the sweet truthful figures of Giotto and Masaccio, and appreciate Giotto moving beyond the limited imagination of his master Cimabue into a realm of purity and beauty. Then we may find more reason and meaning to pursue this life as artist, or just an observer driven to explore the true meaning of life and define the spirit that lies deep within it. We become exhilarated and feel compelled to study life by examining nature and all its profound mysteries.

Young Giotto di Bondone was born in the Tuscan hills of Romagnano, when at an early age he was exposed to the wildlife that inhabited the region. He worked as a shepherd and would draw the goats and other animals he saw moving about in nature. Sometimes he would draw on the rocks, because paper was expensive and scarce. His master and only guide became nature itself. His work became the catalyst for all the Renaissance painters that followed him.

His frescoes would move with great affect the young master Tomasso of Florence nicknamed Massaccio who would be the first painter to depict lifelike figures and movement in his compositions. His work represented nature in its truest form and he was the first painter to use linear perspective. Even though he lived for only twenty seven years his work inspired all of the early painters of the period including Leonardo probably more than any other painter of the early Renaissance.

These years in Italy were truly fascinating ones; the artists and poets would live amongst the ruins and celebrate the beauty and the timelessness that surrounded them. They would take their gifts and create art in a whole new light with nature and virtue as their only guides. Many of these creative men were highly disciplined in several different areas of study and extremely proficient. Some of these artists were from modest beginnings and some of them were from noble family backgrounds of nobility or wealthy parentage, well schooled or taken under the wings of an elder scholar or master of the arts.

If we think back to this time in history we are prone to imagine a crude yet bold environment of rustic and simple proportions but we must conclude that there existed an air of innocence that permeated the peninsula of Italy. There may have been an unimaginable degree of serenity and compassion throughout Italy as well. To visualize these actual circumstances is a real gift in itself, to experience only a part of their whole existence even if only vicariously is a challenge that can be stimulating and liberating to a large degree. When I first visited Florence I was completely overwhelmed by the magnificent historical significance the city holds and the physical remnants that stand as living proof to this period in time. To truly capture some of the precious moments that enabled these great and numerous masters to flourish during this rebirth and begin its development in the north of Italy.

There were of course some very unpleasant realities throughout the early and middle Renaissance period to face as well. Vast populations were devastated for decades by a catastrophic plague known as the Black Death (bubonic plague). It was sometime during the mid fourteen hundreds that a recovery would begin to take hold and the populations would recover creating a healthy working class that was previously decimated. New opportunities began to emerge due to large labor shortages. As a result of these shortages, a wealthy thriving middle class and an elite class of people developed along with a good degree of prosperity in many of the small surrounding villages of Tuscany. Florence became a fertile and progressive melting pot for industry and innovation.

These are no doubt contributing factors to the overall period of growth in fifteenth century Italy. It's very possible that life began to have more meaning, and individuals were deemed more sacred as a direct result of the devastation that the plague placed on the people of northern Italy. We can revert back to Giovanni Boccaccio here with his masterful frame narrative *The Decameron* in which he drew from the tragedies of his contemporary life and the pestilence he bore witness to, which prompted the idea of living in the moment, not in the past or the future. And as a direct result of such devastation the citizenry found real community and appreciation for one another.

One could make the comparison to the aftermath of a protracted war. As time progressed one can't imagine anything too horrific happening in many of the small quaint townships like Arezzo after the years of turmoil and strife that were endured. This was the town that Francesco Petrarca and Leonardo Bruni spent their early years. There in Arezzo a sort of serene warmth surrounded by a compassionate air of tolerance that insulated their early beginnings existed. I imagine there to have been a naive age of innocence that gave way to these superhuman esthetes and created a high culture that would manifest and become accepted by the populous, then nurtured and respected by most of the Italian class strata.

The quattrocento (fifteenth century) was a fascinating time throughout Italy. Florence would enjoy long periods of peace and prosperity between the feuds and foment of the families and villages of the region and that peace would provide the Tuscan city capitol with a solid foundation in which the high renaissance would be built upon. During the middle to late fourteen hundreds, Florence experienced an explosion of tremendous growth and prosperity. It became a center for banking and mercantile trade, a wealthy center for commerce with a robust wool trade surrounded by fertile farmland and abundant vegetation.

There were periods of political unrest all throughout Italy prior to these times, and the wealthy city state of Florence would have to withstand it's moments of instability from time to time as well. Many feudal disputes or invasions by occupying armies were certain to cause strife wrought by the usual struggles for power and greed. There were also natural disasters that periodically occurred in the country, which had some adverse effect on the Italian peninsula as well.

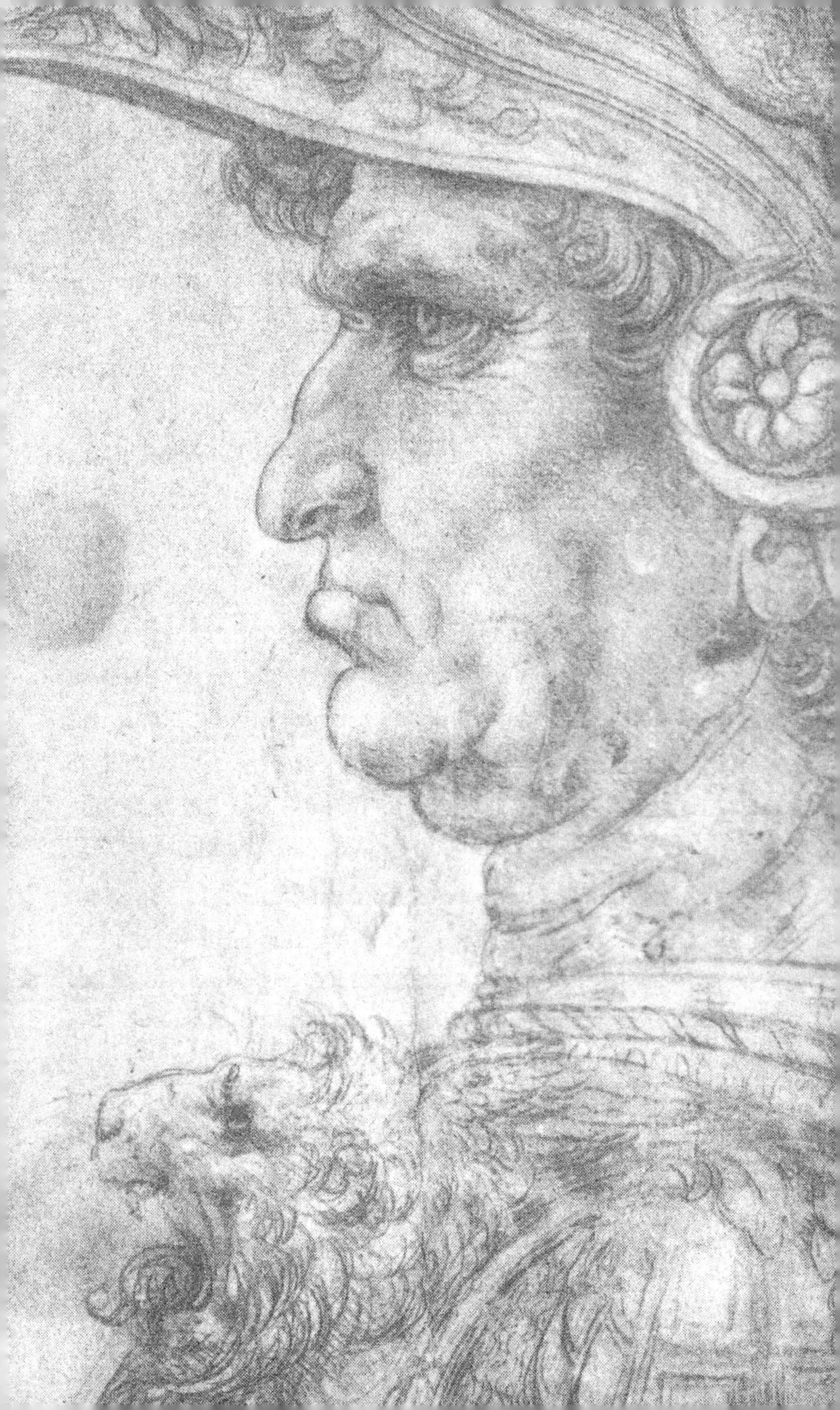

The Proof is in the Peninsula

An unprecedented artistic revolution would begin to take hold the likes of no other known in human history. Through all the pestilence and plague, factions and feuds, the seeds of promise would inevitably be sewn in the fertile and favorable Tuscan soil. There was no stopping its rapid growth and the yield that it would so abundantly produce.

The Peace of Lodi was named after a peace treaty in 1454, two years after Leonardo da' Vinci's birth. It provided tranquility and prosperity to the northern Italian territories and for more than forty years. Milan, Venice, Florence, Rome, and the kingdom of Naples would prosper and enjoy these times of peace. This was a crucial moment for Florence and the Papal States as well, in that the treaty would enable and facilitate a peaceful transition to create the impetus for the high Renaissance.

The Renaissance could never have had any success if it weren't for these favorable times that came about after earlier tumultuous periods. Many talented artists, architects, musicians, poets, artisans and builders flourished during these long peaceful periods. One must take into consideration that most all creative individuals require peace of mind and safety to practice their craft in order to achieve any significant degree of success, so it is easily understood that the conditions became advantageous.

Tangible evidence exists that cannot be ignored. Many thousands of magnificent works created during the Renaissance are still in existence today. There are paintings, sculptures, buildings, literature, and countless other various artifacts that still lay testament to this rich and productive cultural period. One only has to visit the cities of Italy, enter the many museums and churches, and see the great sites of Italy and Europe to be convinced of its success.

All three periods of the Italian Renaissance experienced times of difficulty yet the amount of creative work that was generated and that has survived can never be overlooked. The fifteenth century was the most remarkable and unique century of the Renaissance in that it would garner the emergence of so many great minds, and at the same time promote a creative spirit allowing many favorable circumstances to exist. Florentine life during the Renaissance would eventually lead to an overall happy and propitious environment.

Most of the political strife and conflict during the Renaissance was a necessary but very inconvenient reality that often became highly problematic for the nobles and wealthy businessmen of Florence and the northern territories. For some, it would provide commerce and for others vengeance and purpose. These conflicts were for most of the artists and creative people of the region very disruptive and harmful realities that would inevitably lead to more instability and strife.

However, the facts remain and the success of the Renaissance can never be denied. It's very possible that commerce and prosperity became more important than instability and indocility and the cultured elite more than likely began to influence public policy. There were at times vicious power struggles and some had to rule. One such entity that held the reins of power for many years in Florence and helped to facilitate the wellspring of genius throughout the region was the Medici, a Florentine family known for its powerful and intelligent leadership.

Some say they were medical doctors turned wealthy merchant bankers, and much of the peacetime that I refer to throughout this period that ensued during the mid fifteenth century has been attributed to Cosimo Medici and his son Lorenzo. For a time they would become the most influential and powerful family in all of Europe. The Medici family would then enter the history books by going on to share their wealth and their love for art and culture, and open the massive floodgates to the most creative and ingenious period in recorded history.

As a direct result of their influence many other wealthy patrons would begin to emerge and contribute to the ongoing wellspring of creative talent throughout the peninsula. There were other patrons to the arts of significant renown, for example, the papacy in Rome with Popes Cibo and Julius I I who would grant many commissions during the mid to high Renaissance. The Medici fostered and nurtured an atmosphere of creativity like no others. They enabled many artists, architects, artisans, and apprentices to work freely unencumbered by financial burden.

Cosimo Medici, the eldest of the clan, became one of the wealthiest men in all of Europe. He would contribute a very large portion of his fortune to philanthropy and become an important patron to the arts. He would go on to fund many public works and initiate an academy of Platonism. His son Piero was also a patron to the arts and a collector as well. Piero's wife, Lucrezia Tornabuoni, a cultured and intelligent woman who loved poetry and the arts, would then give birth to Lorenzo the Magnificent. Lorenzo would assume the leading role as head of state after the death of his father. He was a lover of music and poetry and surrounded himself with many of the intellectuals of the Florentine elite. Although he was unsuccessful as a banker he would be remembered for the golden age of Florence and the peaceful times it enjoyed.

At this point in time, Florence would not only enjoy the fruits of its successful trade and commerce, it became the most important city in Europe and enjoyed many festive triumphant moments. There were large tournaments, ceremonies, elaborate feasts, and celebrations that would go on for days and even weeks at a time. Angelo Poliziano, one of the many illustrious poets of the day, would call such moments "blithe enjoyment". These events were a common occurrence throughout the year, and many of them were politically motivated.

The Medici were the rulers of the Florentine people, and to some Florentines the young Lorenzo bore the markings of a despot ruler. Florence was at this time was still considered a republic however, in many ways only in name. The Medici did not maintain any significant titles, only power over the Florentine populous exemplified by their sheer wealth and patronage. They were loved by most Tuscans because of their kind and benevolent nature, and as a result of this, a most prosperous and stable period would take hold due in large part to that great and giving nature of the Medici dynasty and their influence. With these times along came the splendiferous circumstances that gave way to the tides of grace and opportunity which would nourish the formation and growth of the high Renaissance, and with it produce the great artists and thinkers of the age, and the universal man of all ages, Leonardo da' Vinci.

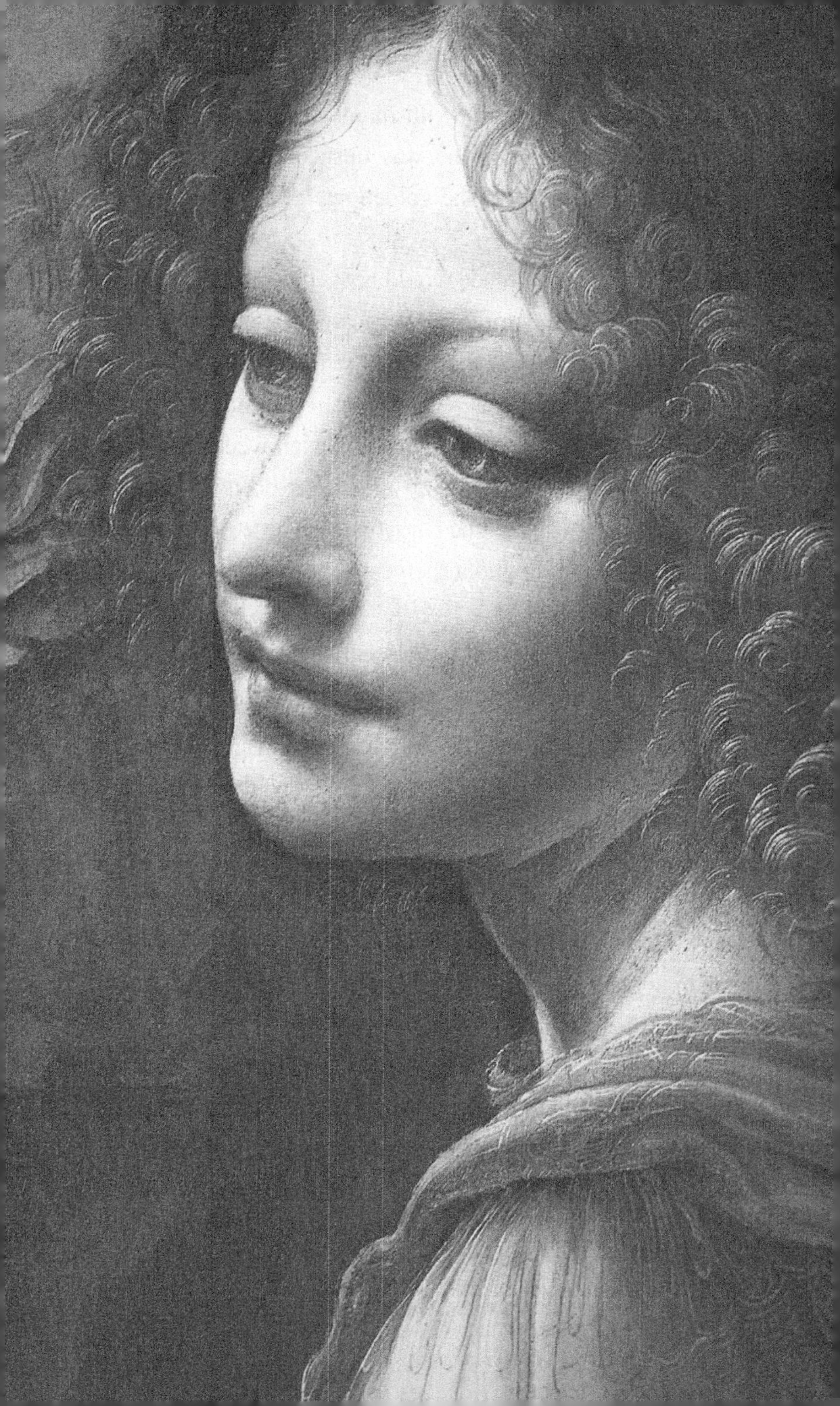

~CHAPTER 5~
HIS BEGINNINGS
- A Dream Realized

LEONARDO da' Vinci was born on April 15th in 1452 in the small rural Tuscan village of Anchiano near Vinci. He was an illegitimate child, considered a bastard or bastardo at birth. However, many believe that he was a child of love and of divine origin. His father Piero da' Vinci, a respected middle class notary (accountant), and his mother Caterina, a beautiful peasant girl, were lovers for a brief moment in time living amongst the gorgeous Tuscan hills, bucolic vineyards, and olive groves of northern Italy.

It is fair to say that baby Leonardo was nourished and cared for by his mother from infancy. Then more than likely due to circumstances of class, she was separated from the young child and he was raised primarily by Sir Piero's parents Antonio and Mona Lucia. It's very possible that Caterina would never gain acceptance to the da' Vinci household because of her peasant status, so as a result the child would be given up to the grand parents and Piero's brother Francesco.

Sir Piero at this time became consumed by his demanding profession and his travels, however he would provide for his family and new child. There is of course the likely hood of Caterina spending some tender loving moments with her young Leonardo during his weaning period and even after the separation during frequent visits to the da' Vinci's, however they would be short lived. There is also the possibility that Caterina stopped seeing her baby Leonardo very early on, due to the intervening grandparents and Piero's new bride Albiera Amadori who became part of the household when Leonardo was born.

Given the loving and kind disposition of Leonardo, who no doubt inherited these beautiful traits from his family, Antonio and Mona Lucia da' Vinci would not eschew Caterina's love for her baby. It's highly possible that even though the bonding with his mother may have been severed and this separation once initiated by her absence would undoubtedly be traumatic; there was no lack of love and affection for the young Leonardo. It's more than likely he was coddled and pampered by his surrogates and Sir Piero's new spouse Albiera. We will never know how young Leonardo handled this very complicated situation, but we can thank the stars he withstood its effect on him.

There may have been a more substantial bond with his mother than we realize when Leonardo was a child and he may have experienced some emotional trauma by sheer neglect. Caterina would soon marry and have to care for two new children. Sir Piero would lead a very busy life and often need to travel more frequently leaving his young son for weeks at a time, so it seems as if Leonardo from the very beginnings of his life experienced some neglect. It is with all likelihood that he was given sufficient love and attention by his grandparents, his stepmother and his kind uncle, but the fact remains, he was cut off from the closest one, his mother.

In the fourteen hundreds the term bastardo (bastard) was something very serious in nature. Having a child out of wedlock was seen as a sinful act with severe repercussions and the child would usually bear the brunt of the ridicule. If you were considered an outcast, there was no getting around it. The stigma was a factor in Leonardo's life from the onset and he was more than likely looked at with disdainful eyes because of it.

However, there is no doubt that he was a special child. As a young boy he would wonder about the small family farm and garden, like any rambunctious little boy and run around the fruit trees and the vineyards in total excitement watching everything with great curiosity and investigating all that moved. He would spend countless hours with his uncle Francesco, who would teach him about the changing seasons, the migratory birds and the wildlife of the region. He taught him about the varieties of plants and trees that grew in and around the hills of Vinci.

Young Leonardo would spend hours by himself playing near the streams and woods of Vinci. He would often invent things using the motion of the streams to propel his ideas, things like water wheels and little boats. He would experiment with dams and redirect streams with bold intuitiveness. There were perhaps countless hours and days he spent as a very young child in total solitude with only nature as his companion.

The oneness that he came to realize with this heavenly environment became his refuge, His total identification with nature would enable him to escape each time he entered its peaceful sanctuary. If he felt much pain at home he could immediately relieve himself from it with a journey into his own private Eden. It is thought that he may have had occasion to visit his mother Caterina who did not live very far from the farm. However one can only imagine these brief encounters with his beautiful mother to be insufficient and heart wrenching moments of quiet desperation.

As the young Leonardo grew older, he became striking in appearance which would no doubt help him in his overall acceptance around the village and with the people of Vinci. There were the warm loving souls of his family who would provide a safe and sound environment for this young and beautiful prodigy in which to grow.

Off in the distance over the lush green hills of Vinci and Vitollini, the town of Florence, a burgeoning Mecca of promise and opportunity was waiting patiently to take this young genius into her loving and warm embrace. The young fragile and spirited Leonardo barely fourteen years of age would dream the most vivid dreams of one day becoming an integral part of something truly great.

However, he would soon realize that being the son of a middle class family and particularly being born illegitimately would present some difficulties. This would not give him many options in the way of a formal education. However his father's success would soon no doubt have some direct effect on his young and extraordinary son's circumstances.

More than likely Leonardo was at first taught the rudiments of grammar and arithmetic and shown how to use the abacus by a priest in Vinci. There was not much to read in rural Vinci; books were expensive items. As a matter of fact, it was 1440, only twelve years prior to Leonardo's birth, when Johannes Gutenberg, a German goldsmith, invented the printing press.

For Leonardo, poetry and literature would have come in the form of folk songs at various occasions, as in times of harvest or Sunday mass. The villagers would read stories from Dante Alighieri, who was the most popular of all the writers during these times. Dante's *Divine Comedy* was read like the bible. Leonardo would not discover the likes of Plato, Cicero, Homer, or Virgil until later in Florence.

It was around 1467 and unlike today, the fifteenth century was a time when an aspiring young artist like Leonardo would first encounter art, face to face in the churches and on the building facades, where he would see the numerous frescoes and many of the sculptural objects left behind by the Romans. They were masterful and intriging works for his young and precocious mind to experience. He would also see the beauty emanating from the newer works of Fra Filippo Lippi, Antonio Veneziano, Giotto di Bondone and the masterful work of Tommaso Masaccio.

Masaccio was Leonardo's soon to be most beloved painter whose work at the time represented a whole new language in painting. He would encounter the creations of the great sculptors Lorenzo Ghiberti, Donato Donatello, Michelozzo, and Lucca Della Robbia. In his early youth he would by inspired by seeing the works of these great masters on an occasional trip to the great city of Florence with his father on business. These artists would help usher in a new age of artistic achievement in the plastic arts, which in turn would grow to encourage all of the young artist minds and the apprentices working in and around Florence.

Leonardo would also observe many of the exquisite artifacts and statuary left from antiquity that was strewn throughout the region, realize its significance and learn to train his eye. His early education was, no doubt, informal yet highly intense to say the least. The many extraordinary artists he began to draw

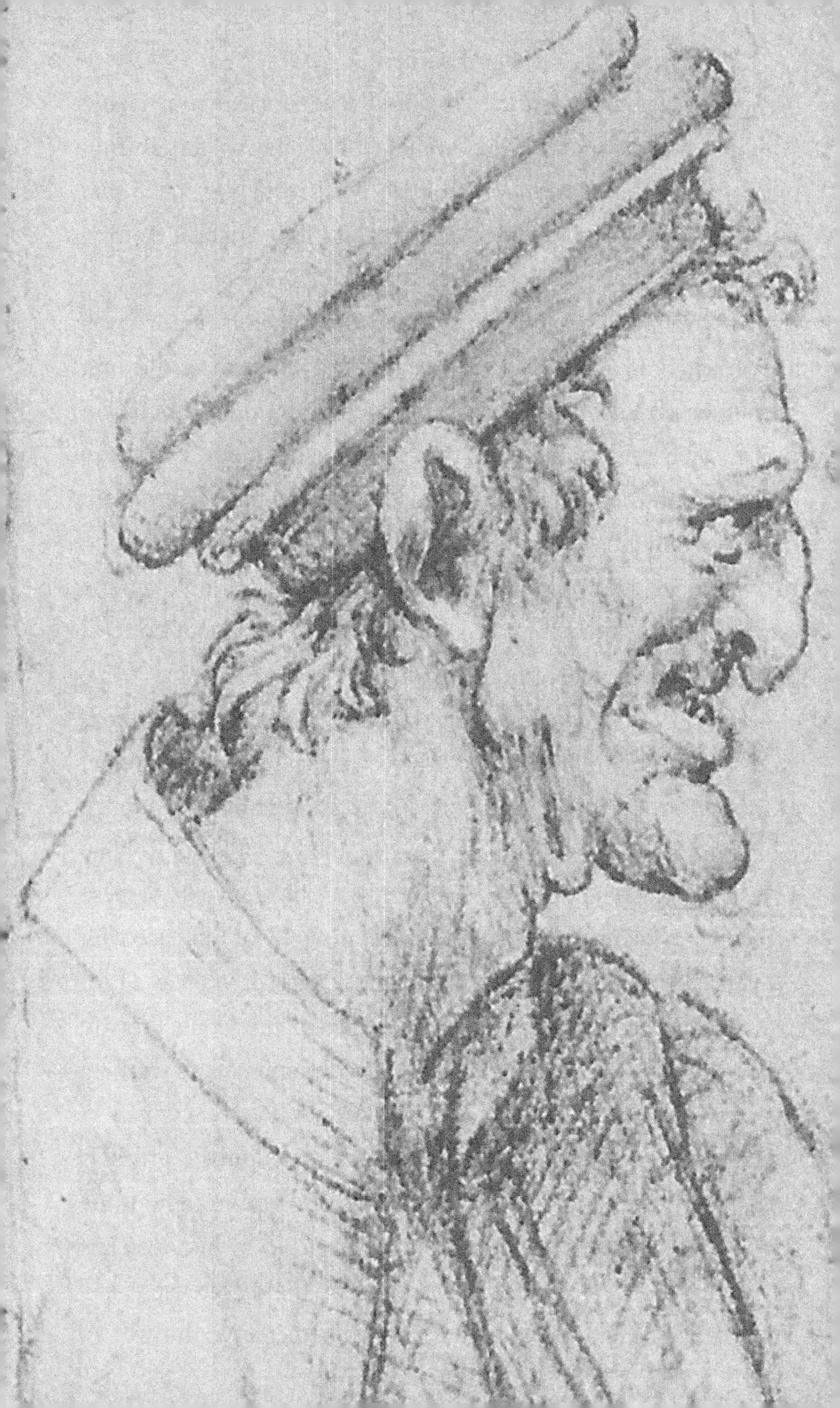

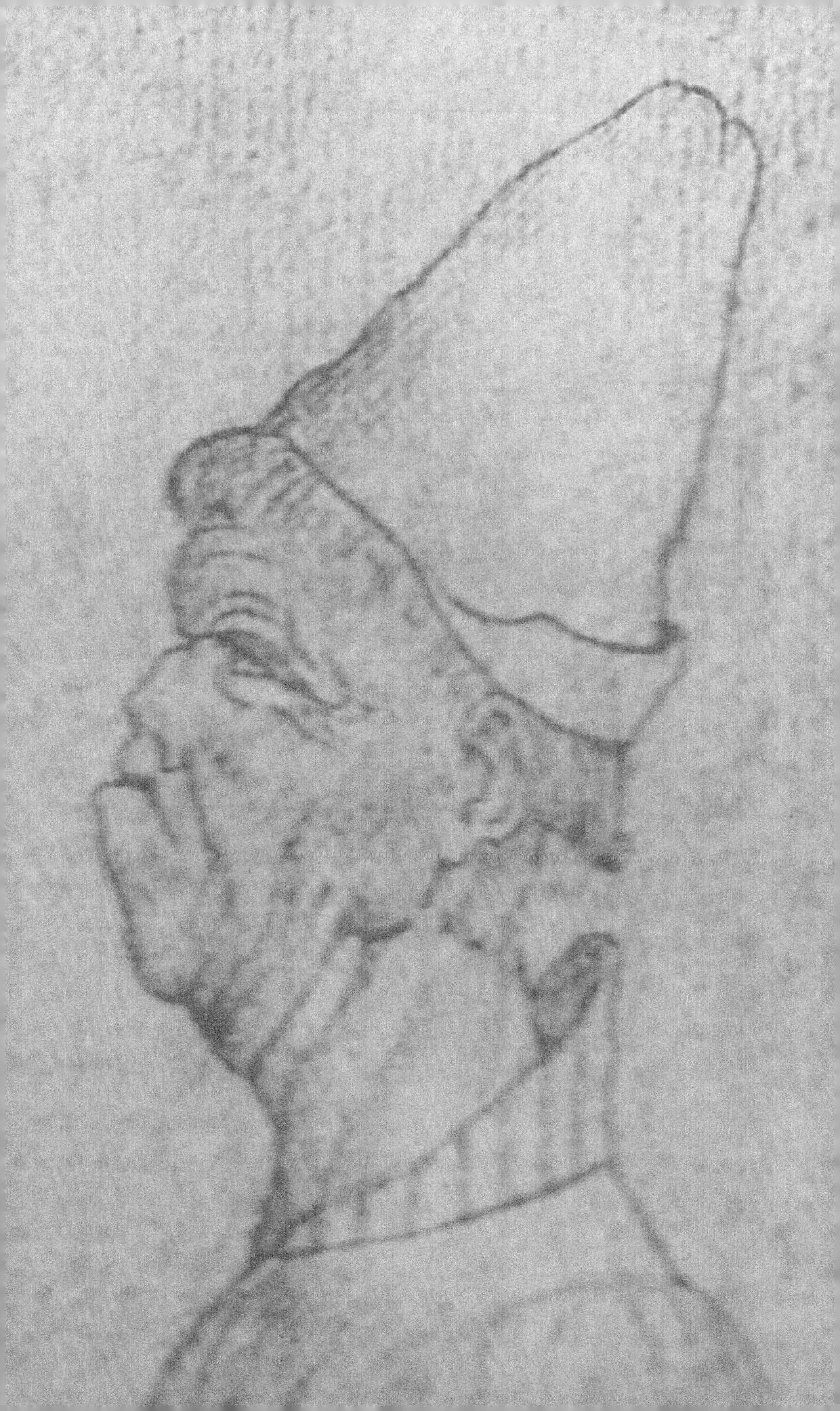

inspiration from would create the basis for his ambitions and lay the course for his future.

As he grew older and his family moved into Florence, there were not many options for the young sensitive and prodigious boy. Carrying the stigma of illegitimacy, many doors would never open to him. No university or public office would ever accept him. His father, thankfully, would secure him a place in the studio of a friend by the name of Andrea Verrocchio.

Leonardo was now around sixteen years of age. Being a boy of good stalk with an acute perception and a sharp intuitive sense, made him an ideal candidate for his introduction into this new and fascinating world. This combined with an immense propensity to create and invent would help to facilitate his acceptance. He would embrace this atmosphere of young creative individuals who all shared an environment of unlimited possibility and promise.

Andrea Verrocchio's studio was a warm and welcoming place for the most gifted and artistic sons of Florence. The workshop would be the place where Leonardo would first learn several trades, develop his skills, and hone each discipline.

This studio was very much like the others in Florence. Each contained many promising young artists silently competing for the many gold florins that lay waiting in the Medici coffers, and in the fat satchels of wealthy patrons throughout Tuscany. However, there was one differing factor; this studio would house a young supreme being who would soon prove to be the most gifted artist in the country; this was Leonardo da' Vinci.

Verrocchio's workshop was a splendid and exiting place for anyone to walk into, especially for the young ambitious and aspiring artists that were chosen to live and learn there. Andrea Verrocchio was at this time a well known master of the arts, and he would provide his young apprentices with all the tools and training necessary to become masters in their own right. However, it would take years of hard work and concentration in order to obtain the highest degree of journeyman and then mastery of each discipline. Andrea Verrocchio was an influential figure during the Middle Renaissance. He was one of the most famous artists at the time; however, he has often been overlooked throughout recent history. Could this have been a direct result of his genius apprentice Leonardo da' Vinci?

Perhaps in the ensuing years he was so overshadowed by the success of his best pupil he had subsequently become dismissed by historians, and considered only as a facilitator to this magnificent prodigy. The fact remains that Andrea del Verrocchio was one of the most important people in Leonardo's life.

Verrocchio was extremely gifted as an artist and as an innovator; he was well versed in many disciplines including music. His sculpture was exemplary, but his most outstanding attribute was that of a true mentor to the many wonderful artists he inspired and influenced. His extraordinary success as master and teacher is clearly visible and apparent in all of his work, and also in the great students work that he nurtured.

As I continue studying the Renaissance, I realize how truly important he was as a pioneer and as an ambitious experimenter. He must have been magnetic to his pupils for his place at this time in society was secure and he was truly a well respected master. We can imagine Leonardo in his youth encouraged by his new master Verrocchio, captivated by his new environs and fully accepted by his fellow apprentices, the likes of Sandro

[illegible]

Credi, Pietro Perugino, Luca Signorelli, and Domenico Ghirlandaio.

Leonardo was around eighteen years old by now and he was a bit older than the other apprentices when he became Verrocchio's first assistant and began running the busy workshop. Florence had become inundated with new construction projects and commissions for most all the studios and artisans throughout the city.

We can imagine the young Leonardo being awestruck at his first site of the massive Duomo being built by Filippo Brunelleshi or being drawn to the beautiful bronze statues of Donatello. And so it was his destiny to arrive at Via de Agnolo to realize his potential and eventually become an integral part of the Florentine fabric, woven with time and patience so as to stand out from the rest as the most sought after artist in all of Italy.

At times my heart yearns for these moments and realities in Tuscany, with all of its beautiful circumstance and grandeur in which these young great souls were born into. Life there was near perfect for a creative soul to develop and become a part of. Throughout this powerful and lasting movement and its expansion, a strong social and psychological community prevailed in Florence. A truly symbiotic environment took hold amongst the townspeople and helped to perpetuate an atmosphere of immense cultural awareness.

Yet it is something we may never know, to feel the splendid warm air of promise, the sanctuary of belonging and creativity living within the familiarity of ones own people, a dream realized. However to think like this is a real luxury in the modern sense and a dream of this nature is for most of us something rather difficult to obtain.

None of us could possibly imagine with accuracy the realities of his life and times, but one is compelled to believe that life was quite good for Leonardo and many of his contemporaries. During this period of the fifteenth century, life was kinder; there was little or no sense of urgency as we know it today, and their perceptions concerning time were much different as a result. There were not many time pieces to think of or rush hours as we experience today. Only long glorious days in which one would walk about Florence seeing the arts and artisans flourish.

Each day these ambitious young men would become totally immersed and engaged in the daily routines of the beautification of their world. They were born into this environment and lived in a creative dreamlike landscape with tremendous energy and productivity in a world right in all its ways. It's like writing this book or creating a piece of art; the pleasures are extremely satisfying on many different levels and at the same time the act of creating seems inviolable and unyielding. The hours pass by like minutes and seconds and the joy at times overwhelming is in the process, and the end result is for the giving.

The bottega, where Verrocchio would train his fledglings the mastery of fine art through tireless moments of fascinating work, was a heavenly place for these young artists. He would explain how to manipulate the mediums of pigment, clay, plaster and paraffin, and the mastery of gold, the interesting techniques of armature building and bronze casting, and the rudiments of drawing, painting and sculpture. All of these young artists would be housed in the bottega; they would work, eat, and sleep under the same roof as true apprentices. Master Verrocchio was also an accomplished musician and would play for his students in between work periods. This is, no doubt, how Leonardo would learn his own mastery of the viol da braccio and the lute.

This workshop, a warm welcoming place for the most gifted and promising sons of this fertile Firenza, this bottega became the crucible in which the alchemy of spirit, mind, and body would meld. It was a place where the eyes, hands, and soul would synthesize dreams into reality. These alchemists turned gold florins into dreamy landscapes, painterly emotions, ideal moments, and created feelings that would depict the most loving circumstances. They nurtured beauty, stopped time, changed space, revealed truth, and brought about promise with the celebration of life.

Andrea Verrocchio's bottega would become a vital component to the high Renaissance. It was a place for all the artists in Florence and the patrons that would frequent the workshops to closely observe the intense creative energy that was omnipresent there. It's ongoing progress, a continuous and exciting formation of idyllic expression, bringing the arts and its practitioners into a realm of unity unlike anything ever imagined.

These passionate disciples would work like bees for the betterment of Florence and Italy unaware of their influence which would one day span the globe. For the Florentine people, there was much excitement generated by this great movement, while most of Italy was looking on with great anticipation and wonderment ready to witness the fruits that these intriguing and fascinating young men would bare, the miraculous production of fine and beautiful works. All the while not knowing that what their great city was witnessing would prove to be the most important cultural period in history.

~CHAPTER 6~
HIS DEVELOPMENT AND SPIRIT

ANDREA Verrocchio's studio became a meeting place where new ideas and possibilities were constant topics of discussion. As these young apprentices matured into accomplished artists they began to exchange new and bold ideas concerning the new techniques and methods they discovered. There were endless discussions regarding the new sciences only recently developed in Italy: topics such as anatomy, astronomy, archeology, botany, perspective, philology, and chemistry. For all of these young artists, life was a celebration of beauty and tremendous freedom to express oneself.

Florence at this time was a city of extraordinary opportunity and the richest, both culturally and commercially in all of Europe. It became a bastion of hope and offered promise of unflinching heroism. These young men would go on to hold positions as arbiters in aesthetics and become important contributors to a civilization which in turn would secure them a place in society and later in history.

These artists would mature into glorious purveyors of true ideals espoused by their humanist predecessors. As this world spun through one hundred years of light and dark matter in its immense universe these brilliant star minds would feel no boundaries, no inhibitions, and no distractions. This truly was a glorious time to be alive, for time was of the essence in the quartrocento and one had time begging for its attention. Time had very little meaning to the artists of the era except that it was to be had. There was plenty of time to learn and to create, and travel was slow by horse and cart or by foot. The Florentines were content with the term "carpe diem" the Latin phrase meaning seize the day. They enjoyed basking in the slow soft tranquil air that permeated their landscape and many of them had little or no use for time, as they knew of it.

Another important aspect that cannot be overlooked is that most of these artists and their apprentices were dedicated to understanding and representing nature in its purist form. It seems as if imitation of the natural world was a noble and worthwhile undertaking. New ideas and methods continuously sprang up from the many great minds concerning nature for these artists, writers, and thinkers living in and around Florence.

These were times of real discovery in Italy and of many scientific, engineering, and architectural breakthroughs. There were great pioneers living amongst these artists, like Amerigo Vespucci and Christopher Columbus, who was born only a few months before Leonardo. There was Leon Alberti with his new treatises on building and painting.

Filippo Brunelleschi who would explain perspective, design and finish his monumental dome. Lorenzo Ghiberti and Donato Bramante together would contribute enormously to the fields of sculpture and architecture.

And of course there was Leonardo da' Vinci beginning his career as the newest universal man. During his apprenticeship he would have occasion to see the great Leon Alberti or Donnato Donatello walking close by, and witness firsthand the glory, feel their soaring spirits, and bask in their success. These great figures would provide guidance and wisdom, even only if from a distance at a ceremony or a special event, for these were the first universal men of the age. They would embody everything great and true to Leonardo and his peers. Their presence was magnetic and electrifying to all of those who stood before them, with total adeptness in all of their pursuits; they were the universal thinkers and facilitators of the age.

All the dukes and duchesses, cardinals, popes, and heads of state were important only in title to them; they held esteemed positions however, only as facilitators for the peace and prosperity that contributed to the artist's livelihoods. As time progressed, Leonardo would gain more responsibility in the studio and he would frequently come in contact with members of the Medici family. He would see first hand the lavish and opulent lifestyle that they lived in. There were beautiful paintings, sculptures, lush tapestries, jewels, and furnishings from all over the world throughout the palaces. Three generations of Medici wealth.

He could see himself living this way more clearly and earnestly. If he felt at all intimidated by them, it would only inspire more ambition and strengthen his resolve to show this exclusive world a truly heroic figure as a great master of the arts.

Leonardo was around twenty five years of age when he completed his apprenticeship in Verrocchio's studio. There was tremendous amount of work for most of the artists in Florence at this time, working on various commissions and creative projects in all the available media. Leonardo would

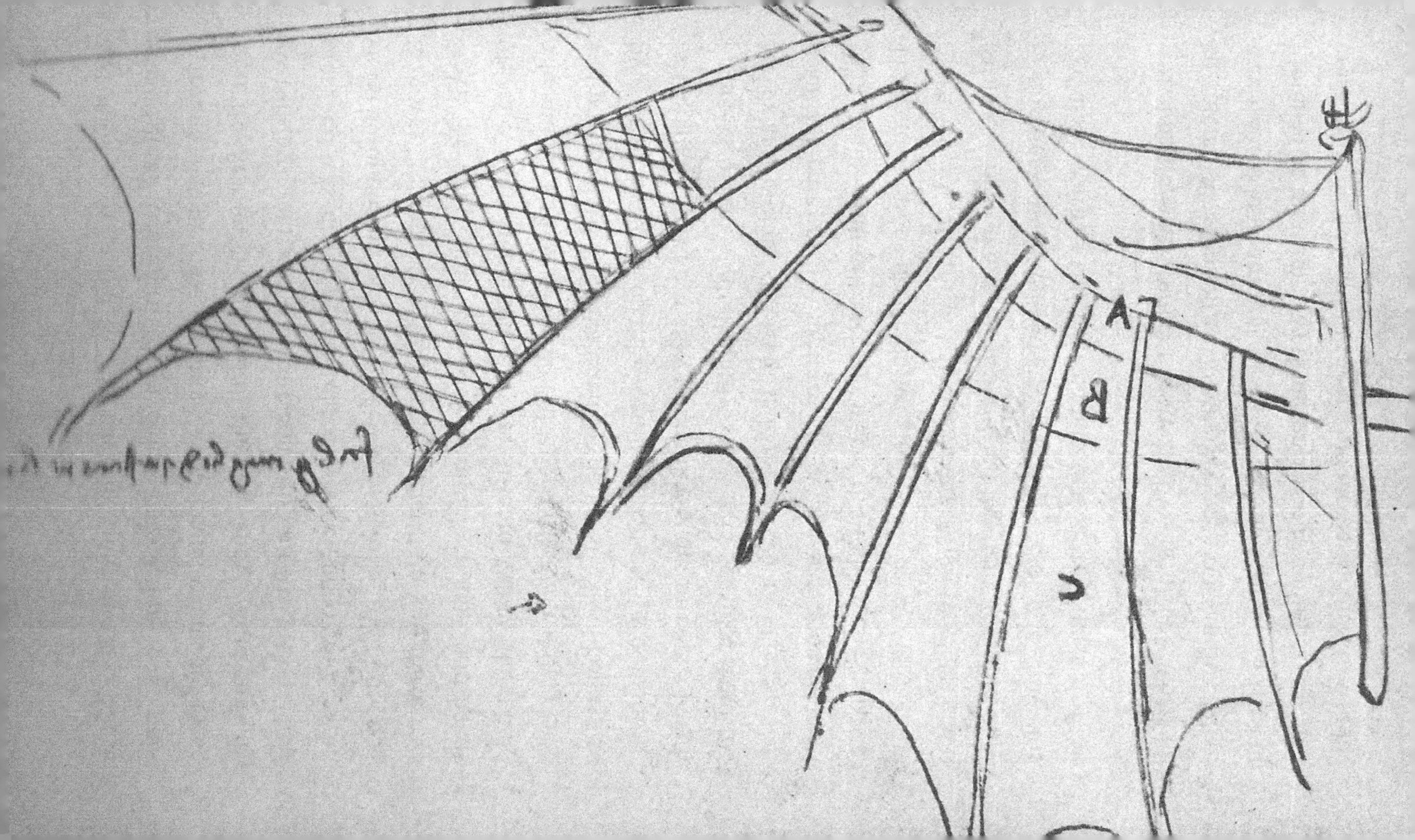

A
B
c

have occasions to visit several of these other artists in town, most notably the Pollaiuolo brothers who had a well known bottega. They were humanist scholars and gifted artists. It is very possible that Leonardo first witnessed Antonio Pollaiuolo flaying a cadaver for his own anatomical studies. This event would no doubt have a serious and lasting effect on the young ambitious genius and influence his future ambitions for anatomical dissection and study.

Another older and important Florentine artist was Paolo Uccello, a painter and decorator who like Leonardo was also interested in geometry and perspective, and Alesso Baldovinetti , an established painter and mosaic artist who invented the egg tempera mixture for varnish. He would provide new ideas and valuable information for Leonardo's chemical research. There were other amazing masters in Florence that contributed to Leonardo's development; men the likes of Paolo dal Pozzo Toscanelli, a genius physician, and philosopher, also well versed in geography and mathematics, and a man named Benedetto who taught arithmetic in Florence.

Many younger artists and friends of Leonardo's from the various workshops around the vibrant city would also take part in the festive activities and at times break from the hard work and disciplined atmosphere of the bottega. Much like today's artists and students in the art schools, having fun was part of the weekly routine. After work on projects was completed or after serious study, the wine, women, and music would take priority.

Sandro Botticelli, a close friend to Leonardo and a practical joker as well, would together with Leonardo cause a stir with a variety of little devious inventions. There was the fabrication of giant balloons using cow intestines that would cause a roar at public gatherings or the manipulation of common lizards into outlandish winged and bearded creatures. I found it fascinating and I could also relate to Leonardo's propensity to act mischievously pulling pranks on his friends and fellow artists, telling jokes and making fun of some of the less desirable's he would encounter.

Many of us have the impression that Leonardo lived a very serious and disciplined life, and no doubt he did, but he also had a rebellious nature about him, hence the clowning and the pranks. Perhaps the stigma of being labeled a bastard had hardened his character to a degree. Leonardo always held disdain for authority and would eventually secure a sufficient degree of protection to avoid any conflicts in his most productive years.

Another interesting fact of the fifteenth century Italian Renaissance is that artists would become members of a guild; in some ways they were like the unions of today. The arts were on a lower scale in society at the onset of the Renaissance however that would change rapidly in the years of the High Renaissance. The artist's guilds served as an important organizational tool for many painters, sculptors and artisans as means to consolidate and legitimize their practices. To the elite class of Florence the plastic arts were initially considered a form of craftsmanship, and painting was a specialty and not thought of as essential as sculpture and jewelry fabrication. Painting was more of a decorative and religious practice. It's fair to say that it became a fine art during the mid to late fifteenth century when Leonardo became its leading proponent, then its master. There were many fresco paintings commissioned throughout this period, however most of the surviving artwork from antiquity was sculptural, hence it had a greater influence on the artists and patrons alike.

Many of the well known masters had their beginnings as goldsmiths and the early to mid Renaissance bottegas were filled with these gifted artisans geared towards making three dimensional objects of decorative art. One very important man that started as a goldsmith and became a pillar to the high Renaissance was Lorenzo Ghiberti, a sculptor, painter, and a collector of artifacts. He was also a humanist and a great innovator. He would set up a large workshop for artists the likes of Donatello, Masolino, Micholozzo, Ucello, and Antonio Pollaiuolo to train in his reinvented process of lost wax bronze casting.

Donato Donatello one of Ghiberti's most gifted students was perhaps the most talented and important artists of the early Renaissance. He pioneered a new language in sculpture and was proficient and accurate in his masterful representations. Donatello was the epitome of the Renaissance artist and was respected throughout all the bottega in Florence. He would unknowingly make sculpting a rational and lucrative occupation and became one of the masters to emulate. He had a profound influence on the young eager minds that observed his great talents and was loved throughout the art world for his kind and loving disposition.

It is again quite an astonishing thing to imagine some of these creative geniuses working and living within the same vicinity.

Just for a moment picture in your mind Pippo Brunelleschi walking down one of the busy streets of Florence only to briefly encounter Donato Donatello and Lorenzo Ghiberti talking enthusiastically with Masolino, Micholozzo and several young onlookers the likes of Sandro Botticelli, Leonardo da' Vinci and their teacher Verrochio, all watching with great anticipation and waiting to join the conversations in earnest. I try to imagine in detail the topics of discussion that took place, or the overall enthusiasms they shared. What it was like on the streets of Florence at this time among these great artists and thinkers. How it was to be totally engaged in this creative and highly productive climate and to feel the safety of identification and kinship of like minded artists. And to the young and impressionable minds that watched these wonderful people turn their world into a place of endless possibilities and beauty it must have been astounding. For the young Leonardo it had to have been sublime.

Masolino da' Panicale was a nickname for Tommaso di Cristoforo Fini, another incredible figure in the early part of the Renaissance. He was a collaborator with Massacio and Ghiberti and he is believed to have created the first oil paintings in the 1420's not Jan Van Eyck in the 1430's as previously believed. Michelozzo Di Bartolomeo Michelozzi, another supreme genius, was a sculptor and architect of the Renaissance. He was a pupil of Ghiberti and collaborator with Donatello. He was also a close friend of Cosimo Medici; who was commissioned to build the Palazzo Medici, one of the more splendid pieces of Renaissance architecture still standing. There was also as mentioned previously Antonio Pollaiolo, a painter, sculptor engraver and goldsmith. He was one of Botticelli's teachers. Antonio was a very accomplished sculptor along with his brother Piero; both of them exciting and emotional painters that were far ahead of their time. If one looks at one of Antonio's paintings, one can easily see the strong influence he had on Botticelli. I could go on and on naming and explaining the significance of these artists, but there were so many wonderful and talented artists flourishing during this time I have difficulty believing this incredibly rich and abundant country yielded so many producers of grace and beauty.

Then I think for a moment and I realize that it did, and there was a need for it. More importantly there was a willingness that perpetuated it. Unlike the realities of today, making art in the fifteenth century was a common occurrence, a rational activity, and there existed no doubts around it, no problems of funding for it, no arguments as to its importance and vitality to society. There are many other important factors that I have discovered in my research of Leonardo da' Vinci and his times that I feel should not be overlooked.

One of these being essentially the total unequivocal realization of mans creative potential and it's limitlessness. Leonardo da' Vinci would personify this thoroughly; he embodied the bold inventive spirit of the age. It wasn't just his inherent gifts or his broad spectrum of talent, it was mainly his unflinching boldness and courage. There were of course the great men before him that laid the ground work and cleared the obstacles of fear and ignorance that the dark ages left behind.

One of these men who came before Leonardo to light his way and inspire him more than any other living being was none other than Leon Battista Alberti, a polymath superhuman of outstanding stature and breadth of mind. This genius possessed a brilliant diamond mind of noble and wealthy origins. He spoke and wrote fluent Latin and composed several outstanding influential literary works; he was an author, artist, architect, priest, linguist, philosopher, and cryptographer. His writings on painting, architecture, family and humanity would influence the entire Renaissance movement.

He was an advocate of Cicero and Marcus Vitruvius Pollio, who was from the Roman era and the first known engineer in history. Alberti would create a whole new approach to the study and application of new principles in architecture. To this day his outstanding achievements in building design and in literary composition are unmatched and remarkable examples of pure aesthetic refinement.

He excelled with blinding speed into high offices and the most prestigious circles in Rome, Florence and later Milan and only now he has been recognized by all historians as the quintessential Renaissance man. I don't know where the term Uomo Universale came from but I am inclined to believe that it was Leon Battista Alberti to whom it was first referred. This magnificent man of the ages would be the artist in which Leonardo da' Vinci would model himself.

Although Alberti was much older than Leonardo he would have a profound affect on the younger genius, Leonardo would also find more comfort in the realization that Alberti was born illegitimately like himself and could identify and feel a kinship with him. Leonardo would finally put away his stigma of illegitimacy and step into a path of unfettered glory.

For Leonardo, Alberti was truly great with his stature well in tact, immense and brilliant and above all courageous in all his endeavors, this universal man would be the one to follow, to venture into similar circles with, working for princes, popes and the like, being called to service for very important commissions, and enjoying a great degree of respect. The Alberti clan, a noble and wealthy Florentine family was an integral part responsible for the success of the Italian Renaissance. This is one of the main reasons I decided to write about the Renaissance and Leonardo da' Vinci. Leon Alberti flourished during the earlier part of the Renaissance. As I learned more about the Renaissance, I became more compelled to learn about him and the tremendous influence he had on Leonardo.

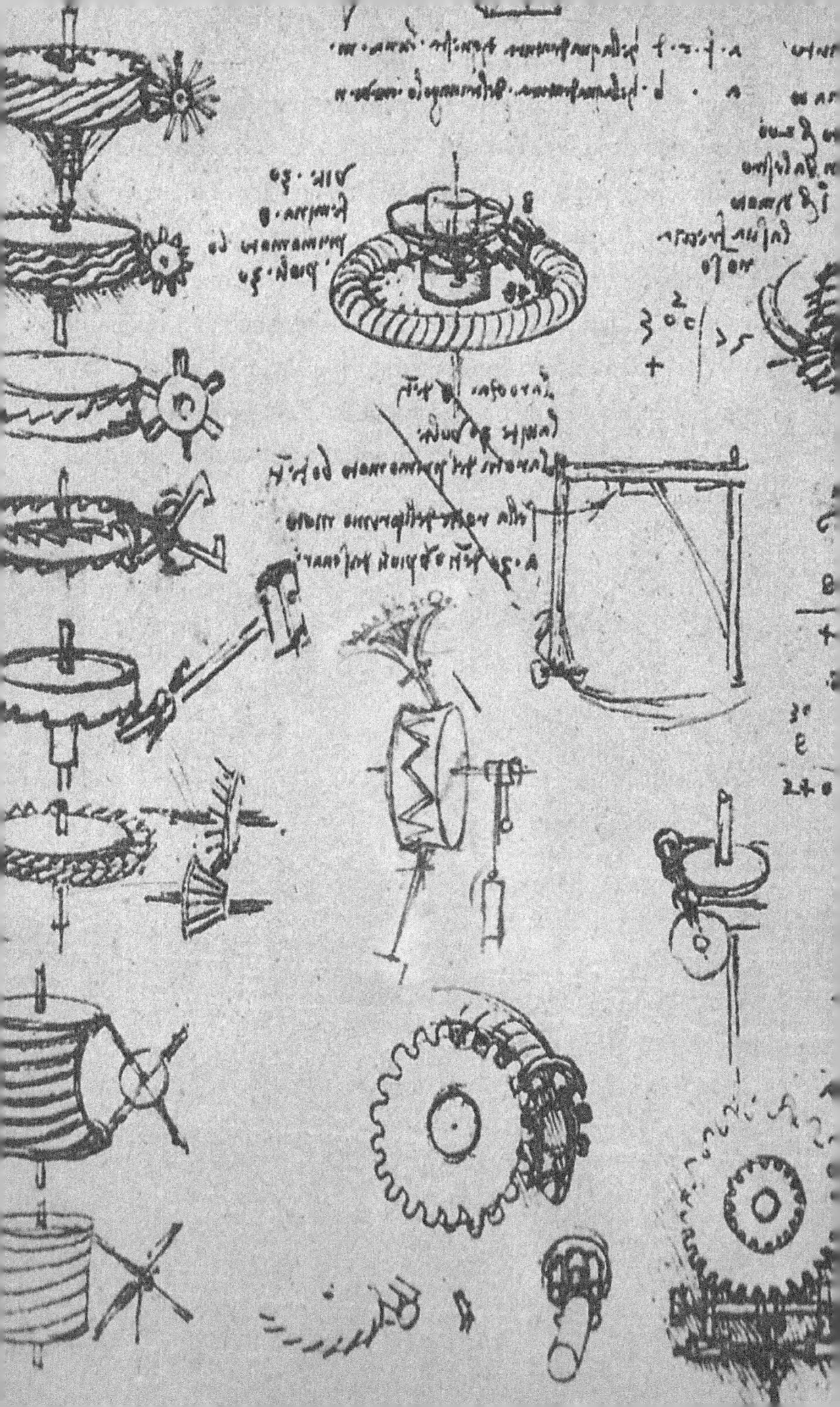

~CHAPTER 7~
THE EMBODIMENT OF GENIUS

I FIND the poetry of Rachel Annand Taylor's intuitive depiction of Leonardo to be very inspiring, and herewith would like to begin this chapter with some passages from her work entitled: *Leonardo The Florentine: A Study in Personality*:

Leonardo was profoundly aware of the flashing singularity of his own mind, a mind ready to leap on any problem and grip it hard through all its changes until it confessed its reality. Ranging at ease through the universe from the infinitely great to the infinitely little. Confidence dwells deep in his speech and actions. He knew he was a many faceted diamond whose mere luster princes might be glad to possess. Yet, with all his justifiable assurance, Leonardo seems not all together at home in the world of mortal affairs. He knows that his intellectual difference from other men is a cleavage that goes to the very roots of life. He is a brilliant efflorescent graft from some strange tree of paradise: he is a dazzling departure from the beaten track like a rainbow bridge that ends in mid air. He is parent less, childless, as if to make him a god had found a peasant girl in the guise of a hawk, not a dove.

Of the ways of the world, he is never quite certain. His spirit is all masked in a beautiful courtesy; but he is often perplexed. And he is not really fortunate. Life, for Leonardo, should have been one smooth, rich experiment, a succession of crystallizing and sublimating stages taking place in a polarized state of impassioned contemplation. But after the fall of Lodovico, existence is all disturbed by catastrophes and irritating contacts.

- Rachel Annand Taylor

During the fifteenth century in Italy, there lived more genius per square mile than that in all of the known world. As mentioned previously, the Medici's were the main facilitators for many of these great people, for some more directly than others. As mentioned earlier the poets Dante and Petrarca were the first important proponents of the Renaissance, Alberti was considered the first universal man who would light the initial path joining the past with the present, integrating the great Greco-Roman principals into a more refined and up to date language and vision.   There lived another extraordinary man, Marsilo Ficino, one of the most influential humanist philosophers of the day, was known throughout Italy for his translation of Platos's complete extant works into Latin. His life long patron Cosimo Medici would appoint him as head of his prestigious Platonist academy. He was also the tutor to young Lorenzo, Cosimo's grandson.

Another remarkable scholar poet was Angelo Poliziano, a student of Ficino's, who would become the tutor to Il Magnifico's Medici's children. Later in the Renaissance period their were men the likes of Giordano Bruno, a Dominican friar, philosopher, mathematician ,poet and astrologer sadly he was burned at the stake for foreseeing cosmic pluralism, (life on other planets) and insisting that the universe is in fact infinite.

As I delved even deeper into my research, I found the close connections of these people in and around the Florentine upper classes to be fascinating as well. It seems as if there was a steady and constant flow of genius that made its way into the bright light of the high court and palatial elite. Most all of these men were actively benevolent advocates of poetry, music, literature and the fine arts. Giovanni (Pico) Mirandola was yet another extraordinarily brilliant man who possessed a massive intellect and literally studied everything available for study in the universities he attended. He became a famous philosopher and taught the amazing capacity of human achievement.

He was also a student of Ficino. Mirandola was extremely brilliant and travelled all over Europe, educating himself and promoting a wide range of possibilities and eclectic knowledge. In addition to his proficiency in Latin and Greek, he also studied Hebrew and Arabic. Later he became a student at Padua University, a center for Aristotelianism, and the University of Paris, an important center for philosophy and theology, which was a hotbed for something known as secular averroism. This term was derived from an Arab philosopher by the name of Averroes. It was based in the interpretation of Aristotle and the relation to their religious beliefs. Very simply put: there is one truth but two ways to reach it; philosophy and religion. Mirandola was known by his friends and associates as the prince of harmony since he believed Plato and Aristotle used different words to express the same concepts. There lived another among many during this period Francesco Guicciardini one of the most important political thinkers of the Renaissance and one of the first historians to document the *Storia di Italia* or (*History of Italy*). He was from a brilliant and noble family; he was another student of Ficino's and a critic and friend of Niccolo Machiavelli.

There are so many more purveyors of fine art and aesthetics that came before Leonardo and lived during his times and after; it would take at least one hundred or more pages to briefly describe them, some I have already mentioned, and others that I will try to mention with some regret for my limited description. There is not a substantial amount written about many of them, and there are many more facts that will never be known to us given the nearly six hundred year time lapse. I try hard to not want more information about them only to be grateful as to what is available.

"The eyes are the windows to the soul," Leonardo once wrote. He coined many phrases that maintain their significance and still hold true to this day. Leonardo's spirit permeates our modern world in so many interesting and delightful ways. Through all of his accomplishments and their effect on our world we can still understand and appreciate the time he dedicated to the cultivation of his soul. Most if not all of the artists living in the fifteenth and sixteenth centuries were immersed in spiritual activities; many of these were religiously motivated; they were practicing religion and painting and sculpting the religious images passed down to them through the millennia. Although I would hesitate to say that they were all spiritual people, I do feel as though the mere act of creating does warrant a certain degree of spirituality regardless of the subject matter.

Leonardo's early work was representational of these religious themes but later he became an exception to those ideas and practices, he was a man of faith but not overtly religious in his ways. I believe he harbored a good degree of distrust and doubt for the men of the church, but not the church itself. I believe that Christian doctrine fascinated him but could not fulfill him as an ultimate and satisfactory system of belief. Some speculate that he was more inclined toward believing that John the Baptist was a more important and significant figure of antiquity than Jesus Christ.

We must take into consideration the seriousness of religious belief at this time in the fifteenth century as well. Most all of the art created up to this time was portrayed in a religious context. Nearly all of the early works that Leonardo had created and collaborated on as a young apprentice in Verrocchio's studio were religious in nature and many of his old friends like Sandro Botticelli, Lorenzo di Credi, Donato Bramante, Luca Pacioli and others were devout Catholics. And there were many more contemporaries like Michelangelo and Raphael who were devout believers. Leonardo was indeed the first one to not only question this authority of the church but found ways of ignoring it without many repercussions. From his early days in Florence when he walked away from a commission to paint the alter piece for the friars of San Donato in Scopeto, he managed to keep a healthy distance from what he believed to be a very stagnant and pervasive belief system.

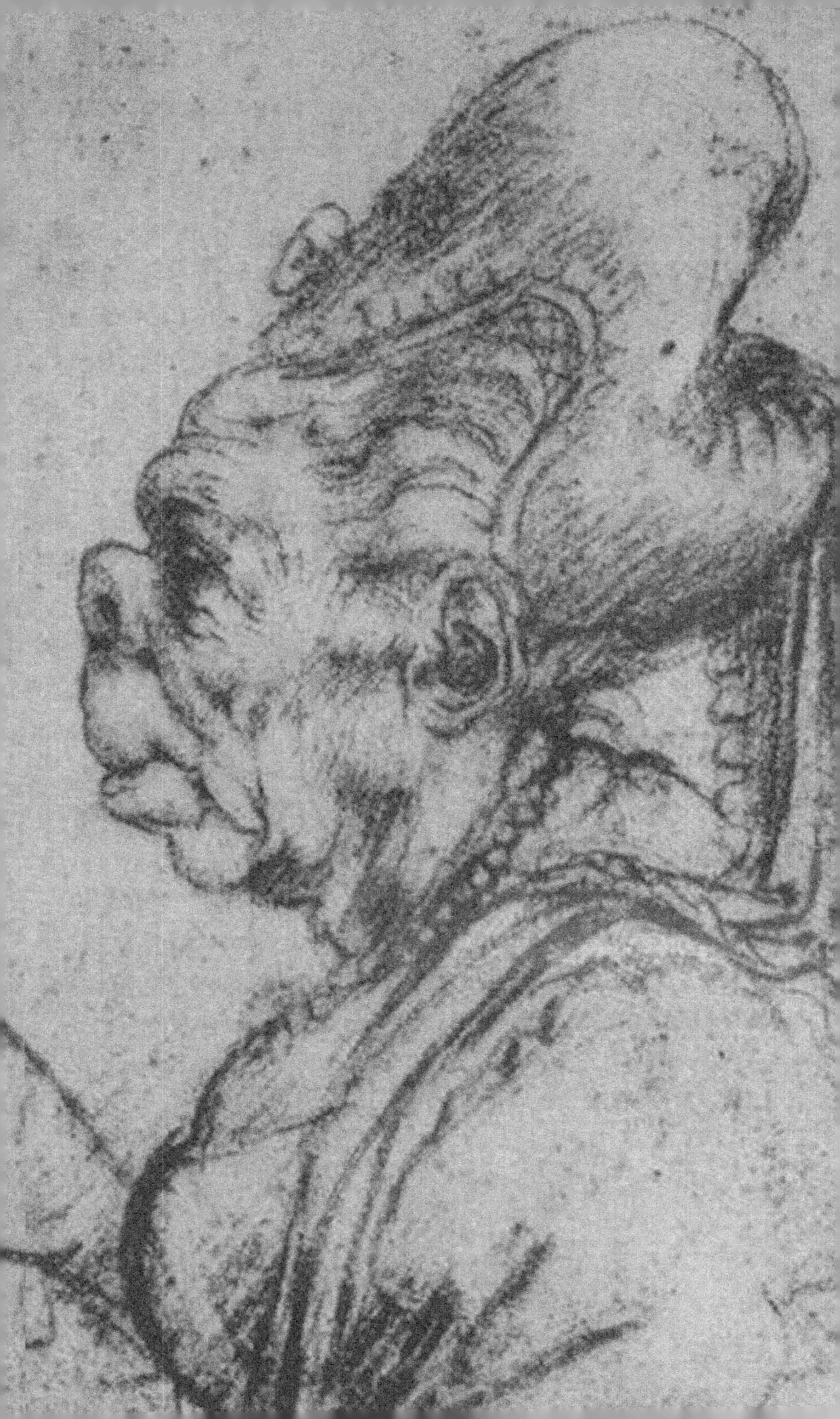

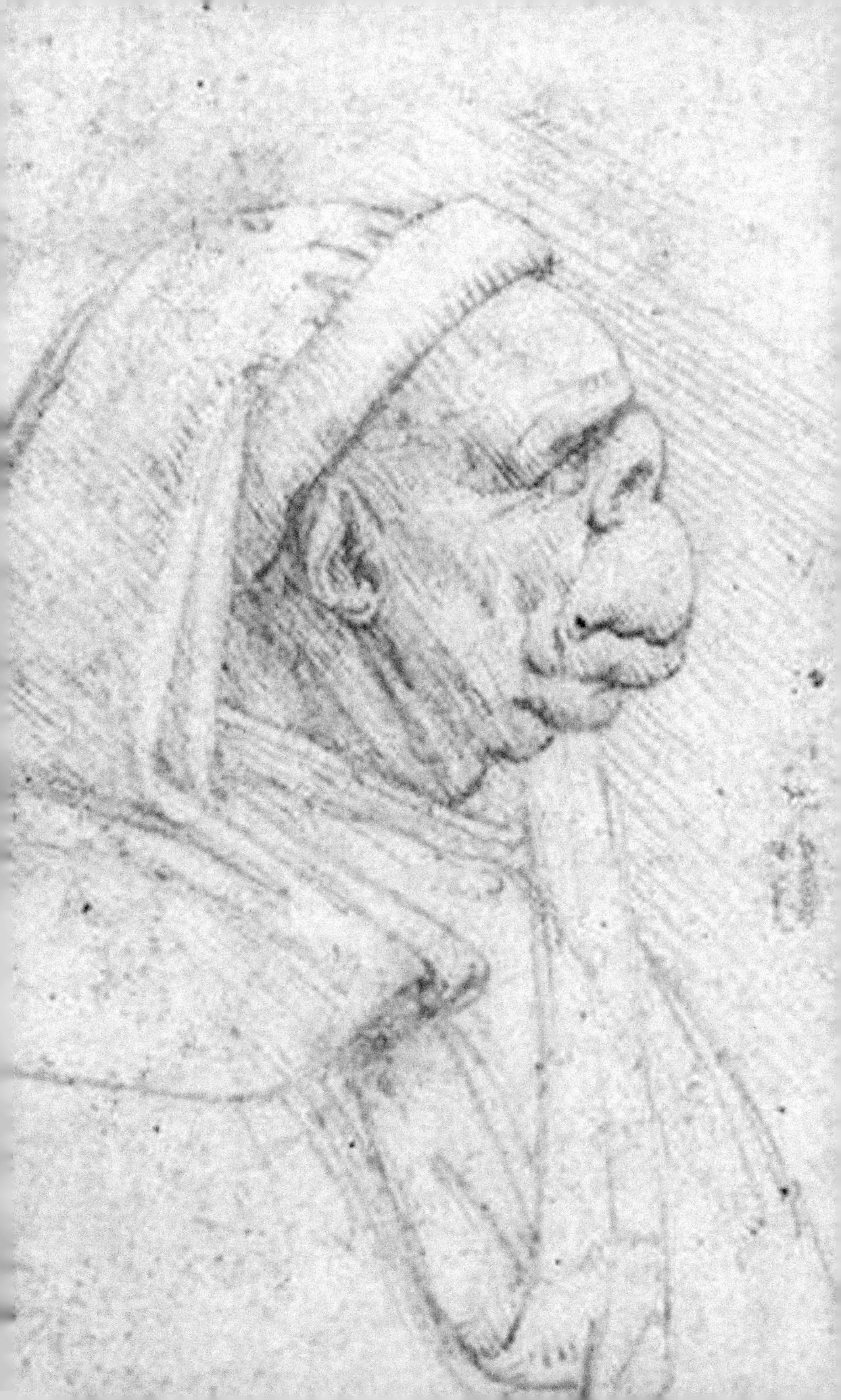

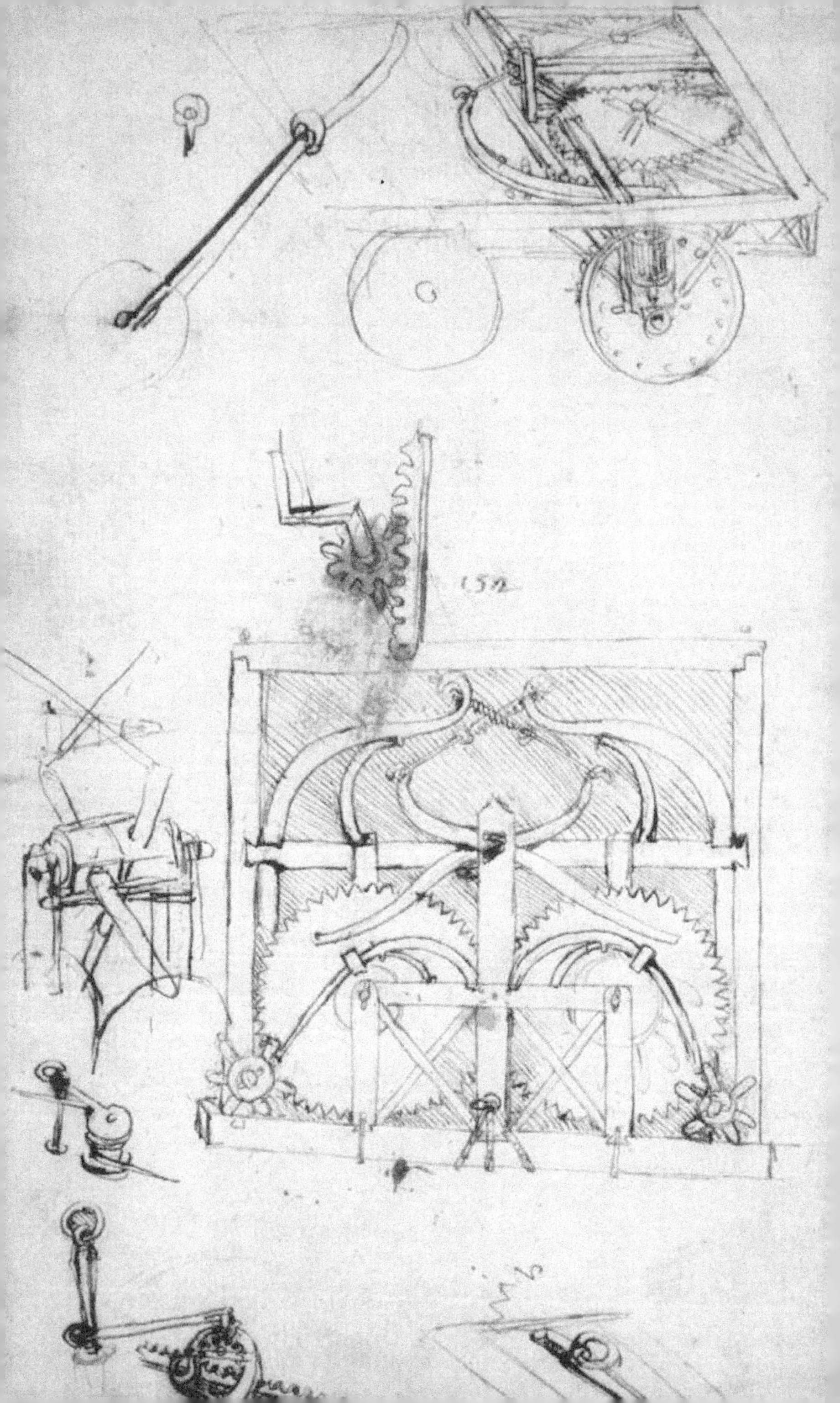

152

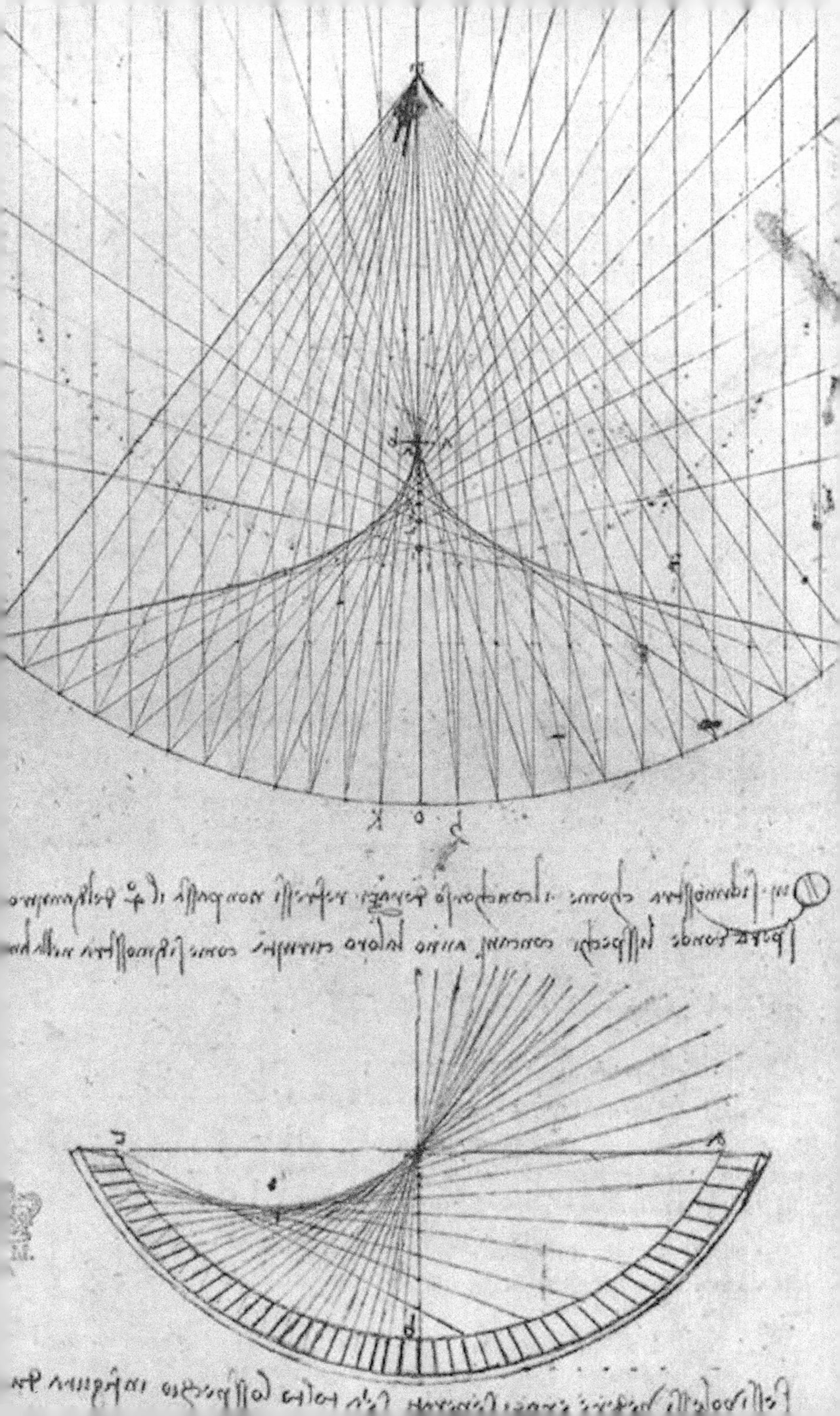

CHAPTER 8

HIS DEPARTURE FROM FLORENCE

LEONARDO was around thirty years old when he left for the Lombard capital of Milan. There are many who speculate about his reasoning for doing so. Firstly his fellow artists and friends Botticelli, Signorelli, Ghirlandaio and Perugino were chosen to work on large painting commissions in Rome, Leonardo was not. Some historians believe that he was asked by Lorenzo Medici to present a unique hand carved lyre to the duke of Milan with the musician and singer Atalante Migliorotti for reasons of political alliance. This sounds quite feasible considering Leonardo was somewhat of a virtuoso with the viol and lute. It is not certain if he played the lyre; however, it is very possible. Leonardo also possessed a beautiful voice. This combined with the fact that music was an integral part and an accepted practice in Lorenzo's court, so it would seem plausible that Lorenzo would use Leonardo and his musical talents to gain favor with his northern ally.

However Lorenzo, who was not at all that close to Leonardo and was more than likely taken aback by his temperament. He may well have been intimidated by Leonardo's energy and extraordinary looks as well. Another possibility is that perhaps it was the religious hierarchy in Rome that Leonardo wanted to avoid. He was after all very independent minded and felt leery toward the church.

Leonardo may very well have contemplated the advantageous

possibilities of working for the wealthy yet despotic ruler Ludovico Sforza, who lead the principality of Milan to a long, prosperous, and peaceful time. He also knew that his Idol Alberti got his start in Milan and went on to receive some rather large commissions working for the prince Malatesta in Rimini. The idea of largess was prevalent amongst many of the princes in Italy and this fact alone may have provided some impetus for young Leonardo's departure from Florence.

We should also remember that Leonardo was nothing really of consequence to Lorenzo Medici, who was always surrounded by various men of letters, scholars and the courts elite. To the elites Leonardo was still a young nameless artist of bastard origin, tarnished by a foolish scandal that no doubt had consequences.

It seems to have been all the more reason for his departure and possible dismissal by Lorenzo and his court. One more fact I thought notable to share is that Lorenzo was not as moved by the plastic arts as he was with music and poetry, but favored Antonio Pollaiuolo as his court painter instead of Leonardo. It's all so fascinating and complex to speculate.

In any case, Leonardo da' Vinci was no doubt a free thinker and a man of his own making. It is again quite an interesting thing to project what we think went on during the early 1480's. Many of us can't imagine this great genius being neglected or mistreated in any fashion simply because of our current perceptions of him and our ideations concerning his illustrious life.

There is no doubt that Leonardo had some very down and dirty moments during these early years, Leonardo was often castigated

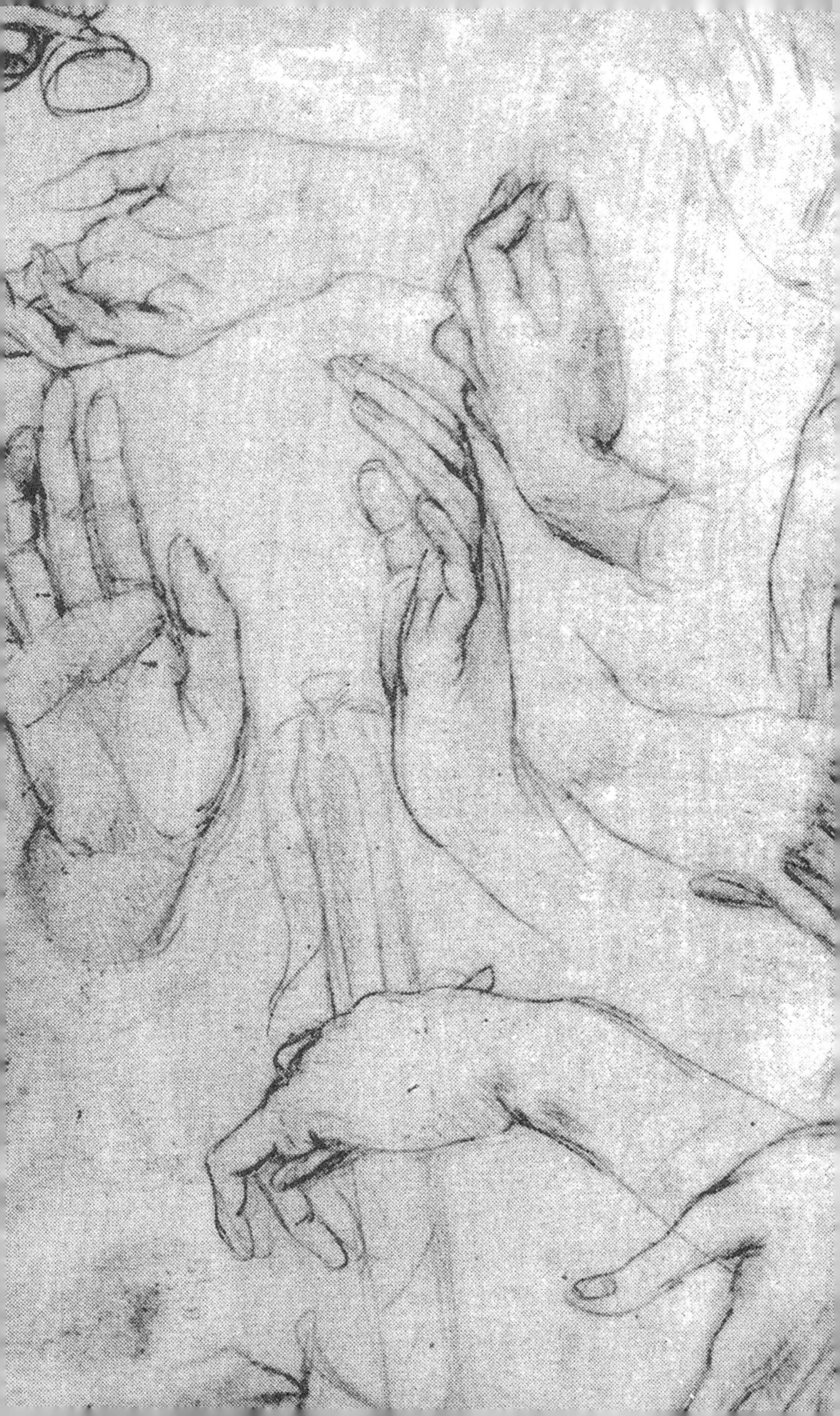

or maligned by his illegitimate status. He was taken advantage of financially and denied certain privileges by the church. There were also moments of mistreatment and unfair practices as well as very fierce competition between many artists of his day.

One more scenario regarding his departure is the speculation that Leonardo wanted the commission for the equestrian monument that Sforza proposed to be erected in his father's name. In any case he left Florence behind for the promising courts of Milano and its duke Ludovico Sforza.

Leonardo would set out on the road to Milan for a fresh start in a much larger city where new adventure and promise would await him. Behind him lay all the years of learning, personal growth, and the joyous moments in his master Verrocchio's studio; the beautiful memories of his loving family, his close artist friends, some of the mistakes he made, and the heartbreak and disappointments he had endured. He would depart as a great young promising warrior with a shimmering sword at his side, heading off to face a great unknown enemy, and one day bring back his conquests.

Milan would soon prove to be the environment of a much bigger industry and broader wealth. On the long road to Milan with his musician friend he would recall all the glory he witnessed when the Sforza's entered Florence during one of their many celebrations. The impressions Ludovico and his enormous court left on his young mind, with their elaborate pomp and riches, celebrating with astounding fan fair, flaunting all its riches and wallowing in its excess.

And so our young ambitious Florentine artist would finally break away from his known world and the people he loved, to venture into a new frontier and to meet new challenges, knowing that what he had in his heart and mind would open all and any doors given the right opportunity.

Leonardo was still struggling financially at this point and there are some years that have altogether vanished from record, finding him in total obscurity. Some historians believe that he was errant and traveled far and wide. Others say he served a short prison term. I enjoy the mystery for all its worth.

There is no doubt that he must have endured very serious and difficult moments throughout his early career, it is evident in his steadfast and courageous character. At times Leonardo would become indignant and difficult to those who did not fully understand his creative genius. He found himself often employed by Philistines and in the service of empty worldliness subjected to certain politics or small mindlessness and working on projects that did not at all hold his interest.

He would first make his way into some of the finer musical circles of Milan by performing with his stringed instruments and his eloquent voice. He began to charm the ducal court all the while knowing that he had no intention of making music his career, only using it as a vehicle for furthering his position and advancing his goals. Leonardo would soon make new friends with many poets and musicians and surprise them with his intellect and wit. It was not long after these introductory years when his great talent as a painter would begin to shine through and the sublime ground breaking masterpiece of the *Virgin and the Rocks* was painted.

Now into his mid-thirties Leonardo would compose the famous introductory letter to the duke of Milan, Ludovico Sforza, espousing his talents as a military engineer and expressing his inventive prowess. However, it turns out that the letter may have never been sent to Sforza, which brings to mind a very important and cogent conclusion in reference to Leonardo's famous military drawings.

We should first take into consideration the realities of fifteenth century Italy and some unfortunate exposure to various violent acts he had witnessed.

All through his creative life he was gifted with an acute propensity and remarkable ability to imagine things, some rather horrific and outlandish things that appear to be bellicose in nature. However, throughout most of his life, Leonardo was always drawing fascinating things, some futuristic, and many scientific and exploratory in nature.

He produced hundreds of inventive and beautiful drawings during these years, most of them descriptive and ingenious works. Many of the drawings are outlandish and fantastic and far ahead of their time, like his predecessor Mariano Taccola, Leonardo was one of the only artists producing many mechanical cut a ways, which were phenomenal and highly detailed depictions of sliced anatomical and mechanical studies. There are now in existence over six thousand manuscripts that include the drawings that became instrumental and insightful to the countless artists, doctors, scientists and historians throughout the ages. The military inventions were very few in number compared to the many beautiful and inventive drawings of nature and ideas. These drawings of invention and nature are some of the most valued and priceless articles on earth.

Leonardo was also a very private man and prone to much secrecy. I seriously doubt he shared these outlandish and fantastic sketches with many people. He possessed a vivid and extraordinary imagination but perhaps these drawings were only about lofty ideas to gain wealth or even just some form of relief given his insolvent status. Many of his sketches are centuries ahead of their times and incorporate defensive strategies to avoid military conflicts, such as diverting rivers and flooding plains. There are bridge designs and ideas for building fortifications and reinforcements. Some of his illustrations like the giant crossbow and the state of the art armored vehicle, the machine guns or exploding projectiles must have been viewed as if they were items from outer space or from the mind of a madman. That is to say, if they were ever seen at all.

So with all of this in mind and his secretive nature I don't believe his military work held much importance to anyone but himself and his futuristic inclinations. So Leonardo would design systems in his own world, and he perhaps did entertain the thought of gaining acceptance through them. He would imagine himself presenting them to the military might of the age and becoming supreme engineer as his great ancient predecessor Vitruvius did before him.

This would prove to be true in the years ahead when he would venture into the path of the violent and charismatic prince, Cesare Borgia. I must confess that for many years I found myself somewhat confused by Leonardo's military designs, I didn't know what to think of this creative genius as military engineer, this wonderful artist and creative genius I wanted so dearly to emulate. Then I learned more about him and realized through my research that somehow many of his manuscripts and important drawings came into the possession of some English swindlers and made their way into the collection of the Q.E.II and her Windsor library. One can observe her stamp that interferes with and perverts the images of this great master to a small degree.. These military drawings more than any others would make their way into countless publications all over the world and promulgate a dark and perverse nature that is unfortunate and has contributed to a negative twisted perception towards him.

Now during the nearly two decades of Leonardo's presence in Milan the house of Sforza would cast a blaze of unprecedented magnificence over the Italian peninsula. It's wealth not only seen as material wealth but intellectual and artistic richness that created a cultural melting pot of endless possibilities. This is where the Florentine from Vinci would take his cue and put his talents to the test.

Milan would become his second home and the place he would flourish as an innovator and artist extraordinaire. This is where he would bring into existence most of his greatest works and make his name. It was now 1493 and after years of cultivating relationships and gaining favor in the ducal court Leonardo would unveil his clay colossus model of the *Gran Cavallo* (the great horse) statue, almost eight meters in height, standing immense, dynamic and mighty. It was received with total amazement, and his fame as a sculptor would reverberate through every village in Italy and beyond. This colossal work of sculpture would solidify Leonardo's status as a great artist.

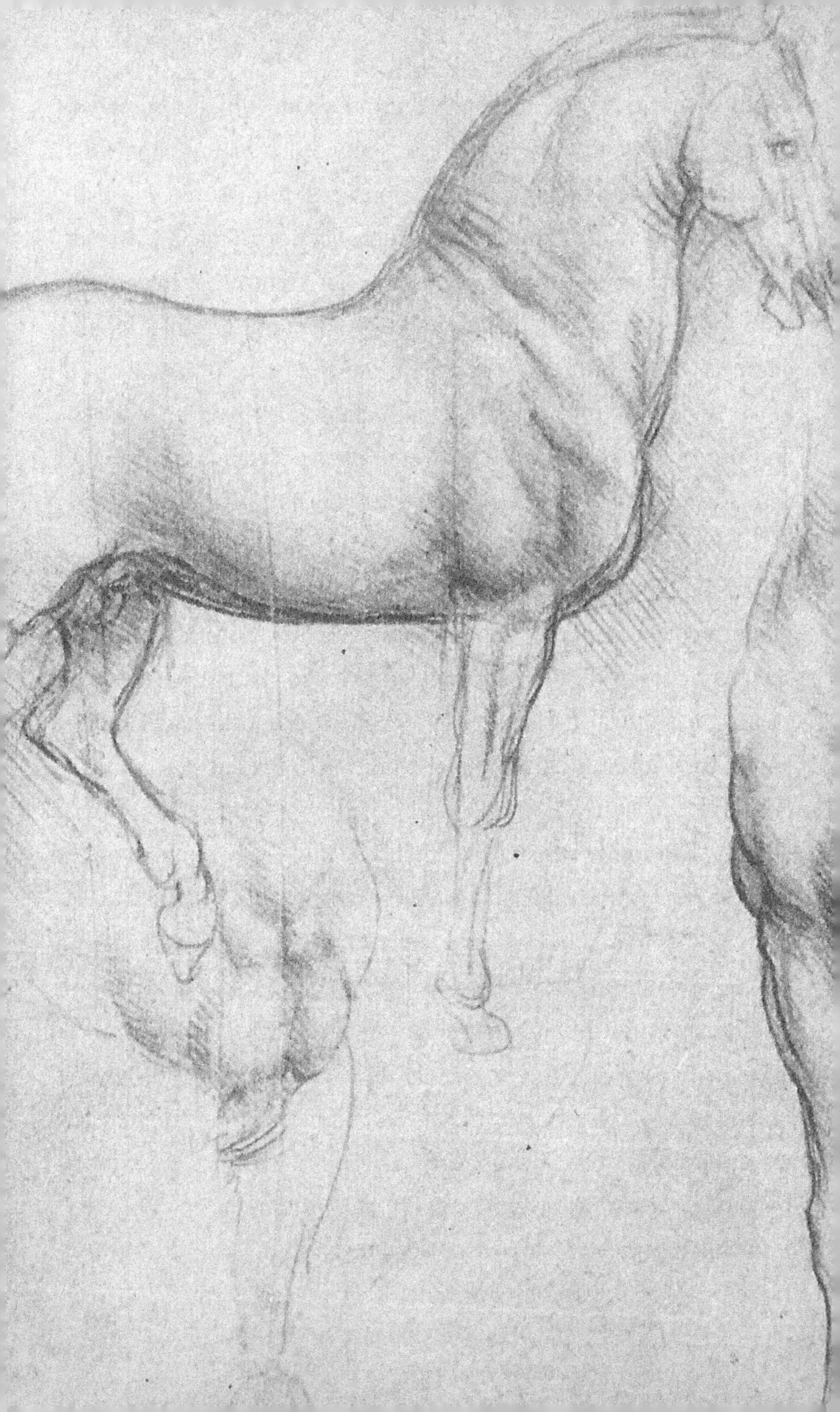

The early years with his master Verrocchio and the great talented sculptors of Florence who influenced him had finally paid off, and his dreams as an accomplished sculptor would be realized in this enormous three dimensional masterpiece. He was now coming into his own. His name was in nearly every home in and around Milan. His place secured, and his vision for himself and his position more satisfactory.

It was around 1495 and there was some intense military activity beginning to occur on the northern borders of Italy. Leonardo would be engaged as military engineer in the designing and casting of mortars and cannons. Things were still reasonably stable in northern Italy.

However the black plague would rear its ugly head once again and kill over fifty thousand people in the northern territories. Sometime during these years Leonardo was commissioned to paint *The Last Supper*, a painting that has been considered one of the most important works of art ever created. Leonardo, naturally and adroitly was simultaneously working on many building projects, there were churches and cathedrals, also an incredible multi leveled city for Ludovico. He would design incredible machines for the textile industry and produce elaborate set and costume designs for the duke as well.

One of the court poets Bellincione would praise Leonardo for his ingenious set designs and the mechanisms he created. He would soon come in contact with the pioneering work of Filarete, the influential architect, and Francesco di Giorgione a prominent and extraordinary artist in his own right. There is so much we don't know about these years and the extraordinary men that flourished during Leonardo's time as I stated earlier.

There are so many written layers of fact and fiction, speculation and fabrication that it's mind bending. We do have much of the physical evidence, but the time lines are incredibly difficult to deconstruct and render adequately. It is mystifying and astounding to say the least. We must, however, take into consideration the fact that Leonardo would always have assistance at his disposal, among the many there was Marco d'Oggiono and Giovanni Antonio Boltraffio and his newly adopted son Giacomo Ferrara whom he called Salai for his diabolic disposition.

Leonardo possessed a strong will and noble character. He was not at all consumed by wealth and riches but enjoyed living well and having nice things, such as good food, fine horses, beautiful clothes and splendid lodgings. Leonardo was always generous at heart and with his rewards he shared much with his pupils, friends and family.

We don't know much at all about his studio in Milan. We do know that he was a perfectionist and would oversee and take part in all the work that came out of his workshop, there were many works commissioned by the duke and his court for various celebrations that were disposed of; such as objects and props for stage performances, things like painted fabrics and backdrops, masks and mechanical contraptions. Leonardo worked tirelessly and consistently and was adept in every way imaginable. However, documents around this time were sparse and Leonardo's life would soon change profoundly once again, when he entered the world of academia and the University of Pavia where he immersed himself in the research and writings of many profound thinkers.

He found himself among the most extraordinary minds in all

of Europe. The names of Marco Antonio della Torre and one Fazio Cardano were just two of several dozen great scientific thinkers of the day. There were breakthroughs in geology and anatomy, mathematics and philosophy. Leonardo would emerge as a scientist and a thinker second to none. His audacity and level of confidence must have been mind altering at this time. He could bring to the table of knowledge and to his prestigious academicians far more than they could handle.

His broad experience in so many varying fields of study with so many great thinkers and experimenters would put him light years ahead of them. His intuitive perceptibility was astonishing. He was not only well versed in historical documentation but he became a philosopher and a great thinker and a man of original thought. He was more than likely known throughout the university at this time for his mastery of the arts first and foremost and his great work in the ducal court of Milan.

He would soon leave Pavia with a broader understanding of the world of science and technology and apply even greater knowledge and wisdom to his studies. And when he looked back at Milan he would internalize only one regret; the great Francesco Sforza monument he left behind and never completed as initially planned. He was perhaps stretched far beyond his own incredible limits by the extraordinary demand on his person. The external pressures and time constraints presented by his perfection driven man.

If perhaps he were understood more and given more resources the *Gran Cavallo* would stand today. He was asked to complete too many tasks at once and found himself at times so immersed

in new and uncharted territory that it became extremely difficult to separate his time from them and to take up the paint brush once again and feel servile and bored by the familiarity of its processes. And yet his most important task would never come to fruition. All of his delightful and charming sketches of the great horse and his ingenious casting techniques would never be tested until many centuries later.

In 1490, the tide would soon turn for the Milanese court and all of its greatness. Things began to falter and the long period of astounding growth would come crashing down. His patron and illustrious duke Ludovico would go into hiding, ousted by Louis XII of Ligny and his French army. Leonardo would be forced to move on, knowing what he had left behind would not be in vain.

He would look back on many years of tremendous personal growth and success with a sense of confidence in his abilities that would no doubt lead to new opportunities elsewhere. He was now financially set and could freely travel with his entourage and pupils. Leonardo would soon cross paths with a Franciscan monk by the name of Lucca Pacioli, a disciple of Alberti's and Piero della Franceca's. Pacioli was a teacher of mathematics and a theorist, also a writer and considered to be the father of our modern day accounting system. He would become an important part of Leonardo's development as a mathematician.

They would travel around northern Italy inspiring each other to new heights and would soon collaborate on a book entitled *De Divina Proporsione*. It seems more than likely that Leonardo had a great influence on his friend Lucca, thus he contributed more than most historians realize. There is no doubt that Lucca's positive affirmations and friendship towards Leonardo would account for the book's completion and success.

The effect these close friends had on each other must have been truly immense. There may have been many breakthroughs and new theories and formulations that were discussed but never put into writing as was the case with so many of his intriguing relationships. We should be grateful for the work that was documented and passed down to us and is still being used today.

I can only imagine the depths in which these two intellectual giants were engrossed, creating the first mathematical treatise on accounting and some of the astounding theories and conclusions that were drawn in reference to a modern day mathematics that was hundreds of years ahead of its time.

Leonardo was now a well respected and famous artist, scientist, engineer and self made scholar, who could pay his way with all his pupils and colleagues, enjoy the many fruits of his labor and move in total freedom. He received admiration everywhere he traveled. He would soon find himself in the service of the General and Prince Cesare Borgia, a bastard son of Pope Alexander, one of the most despicable popes to ever hold the title.

Pope Alexander VI Borgia was not Italian, he was Sephardic and he was no doubt evil and malicious in all his ways. He provided his son Cesare the title and prominence over a large army. As the son of the powerful pope he was brilliant yet ruthless and much that has been written about him is quite negative, some would say for good reason. His sister Lucrezia was also known throughout and would be instrumental in several of his conquests with her ruthless and deceitful ways. With her manipulations, she would help her brother to gain and secure power.

Cesare would become respected and acclaimed in some of the

small townships for directing most of his aggression towards despots and oppressors and bring a degree peace to many villages throughout central Italy and establish a civil magistrature. However for many others he was a megalomaniac, violent and ruthless in his ways with a bent for inflicting serious pain on his enemies.

There may have been a moment of naive respect between the great and bold artist / engineer and the audacious prince, both of them striking in appearance, highly intelligent and independently minded. They were both born illegitimately and had a scorn for convention. For seven or eight months Leonardo traveled independently of Cesare's army, examining fortifications, mapping the regions and executing plans for redirecting waterways and creating diversions for defensive strategy.

I'm sure for Leonardo there was a good degree of infatuation by this spectacle of avarice and mayhem. Cesare was a complex and striking militant prince, a tyrant leader, he possessed a bold and uncompromising nature, void of hypocrisy but prone to inflict mass casualty and chaos. At some point during this brief and fascinating adventure Leonardo could not help but see firsthand what helped to bring this young 27 year old prince to power. The sensitive and laconic master would inevitably become repulsed by what he had to witness in the coming months which would inevitably expedite his departure.

Another intriguing figure that would arrive on the scene was that of a small man with short hair, malicious eyes and a brilliant mind. This was Niccolo Machiavelli, the secretary of the Florentine republic sent to Borgia's camp in Romangna to observe the enigmatic prince and eagerly send the Tuscan authorities word of Borgia's puissant triumphs. Machiavelli was a brilliant writer and poet, a theorist and the first man in history to objectively study mankind and his passions in a thoroughly dispassionate way.

He aspired to no political doctrine and his book entitled *The Prince* is believed to be inspired by Cesare Borgia and had great influence on men the likes of Napoleon Bonaparte among many others. There is no doubt that Leonardo was quite captivated by this young and brilliant little man. Machiavelli without question knew of Leonardo's great reputation and the two men would undoubtedly spend several hours over late night fires in discussion and analysis of the problems at hand.

In the coming years Machiavelli would help Leonardo in securing several commissions. One in particular was a massive operation that entailed the redirecting of the Arno River. I can't speculate about their relationship further, however from the information I have gathered I believe Leonardo did not hold Machiavelli in the highest of esteem. My intuition tells me that Machiavelli's beliefs though complex and aggressive did not coincide with the great and sensitive humanist views of the creative Leonardo. Machiavelli would eventually be ousted from public office and at one point he was tortured and exiled for his beliefs. His name would go down in history as one of the most controversial figures in history.

Leonardo would eventually end up in Florence working on several projects concerning mathematics and flight; he would oversee his pupils to some degree and work on several small portrait paintings, one of them very possibly the *Mona Lisa*. His studio at this time was quite busy although haphazard and seeming as if it were being run from day to day. I have no doubt that Leonardo found it very difficult and indeed distracting to delegate and prioritize certain tasks given his natural inclination to engage himself in some of the most advanced studies and work known to man. He probably had ample studio space for his pupils, as well as his own private research and study, but would often spend times uninterrupted. With almost complete abandonment for his immediate surroundings he would continue to create masterful paintings with total precision and care.

~CHAPTER 9~
THE ARTISTS' ARTIST AND MASTER

LEONARDO was 61 when he was summoned to Rome by Pope Leo the X, who became pope Julius II's successor. Leo was one of the Medici clan and the youngest son of Lorenzo. He was not unlike his family in that he supported the arts and sciences. He enjoyed living well and had much respect for Leonardo his elder and famous master from his hometown.

This was a fascinating time in Italy to say the very least. While Leonardo was revered everywhere in Italy and his reputation far reaching, he found himself in Rome surrounded by some of the most extraordinary figures of the high Renaissance. The city had changed dramatically; specifically, the Vatican, since Pope Sixtus's departure and Leonardo's last and perhaps his only previous visit.

There was an abundance of talent and work underway to be seen by the great Florentine master. It must have been mesmerizing for his magnificent mind to absorb, all of this activity and progress knowing that these young masters were thriving in a large part because of his efforts. But it's more than likely he was not at all aware of what he was responsible for, his exploits and his momentum had thrown the quartocento into the highest of gears, and caused a frenzy of creative development that became manifest in all ways of goodness and productivity.

One can't help but to imagine Leonardo's initial response to the ongoing heroic work of Michelangelo in the Sistine Chapel. Perhaps he stood silent, speechless for the shear glory and effort he was witnessing. Now he would realize what this young and passionate genius was truly capable of. It wasn't enough that Michelangelo created his colossus *David* from a massive block of marble, one of if not the most beautiful sculptures ever to be conceived and created. This young master was driven beyond words to show off his God-given talents by painting an extraordinary work of genius on the 68 foot (21 meter) high vaulted ceiling of the Sistine Chapel.

To this master of the universe Leonardo da' Vinci, this may have been perhaps the most significant moment between the two greatest Artists of the Renaissance. A triumphant spectacle of human achievement and of sublime realization in this fifteenth century light of supreme passion for creative achievement and reason. When an artist produces for an artist, he pays the ultimate complement.

He displays his love and respect for his Masters approval. This is what I believe, as an artist, to be one of the most vital and enriching experiences in life. To experience recognition and confirmation of one's own creative achievement and attempt at perfection. This is also one of the most important aspects of all Italian Renaissance art and the key reason for its longevity and importance throughout history. The passionate humanistic qualities inherent in the art created, and the bold execution and love for the processes that were passed down through the ages.

Michelangelo Buonarroti was a man of great emotion and passion but unlike Leonardo he was prone to fits of rage and would at times even appear unkempt. He would work at times nonstop on his sculptures and on the Sistine ceiling. There were extremely long arduous and laborious days and months unrelenting and magnificent, that took place at the Vatican. The young Renaissance master had taken Rome by storm and his presence there was unavoidable.

To Michelangelo, Leonardo appeared to be a man of elegance and refined tastes who traveled in secluded circles and seemed to have no allegiance to anyone but himself. Michelangelo's respect for Leonardo, who was his senior by about fifteen years, was apparent and this master Leonardo would no doubt have to acknowledge Michelangelo's genius. The master was without a doubt the case with another shooting star of the times, whose name was Raphael.

He was a much younger artist than Leonardo but he had the utmost respect for his distant contemporary. Raphael Sanzio da' Urbino was living the life equivalent to a modern day rock star. He had a great studio in Rome with nearly fifty pupils and artisans working on various projects and commissions. He was loved by many because of his immense talents and his kind disposition. Raphael was a masterful painter who studied Leonardo's work intensely.

One only has to see one of his paintings in person to understand how truly special he was. His work is the embodiment of pure beauty and again one can see the evidence of Leonardo's influence very clearly in the portraits that he painted. He worked with such precision and passion, and he portrayed emotion with great effect like Leonardo and Massacio before him. His paintings are bright in color and dynamic in structure, his

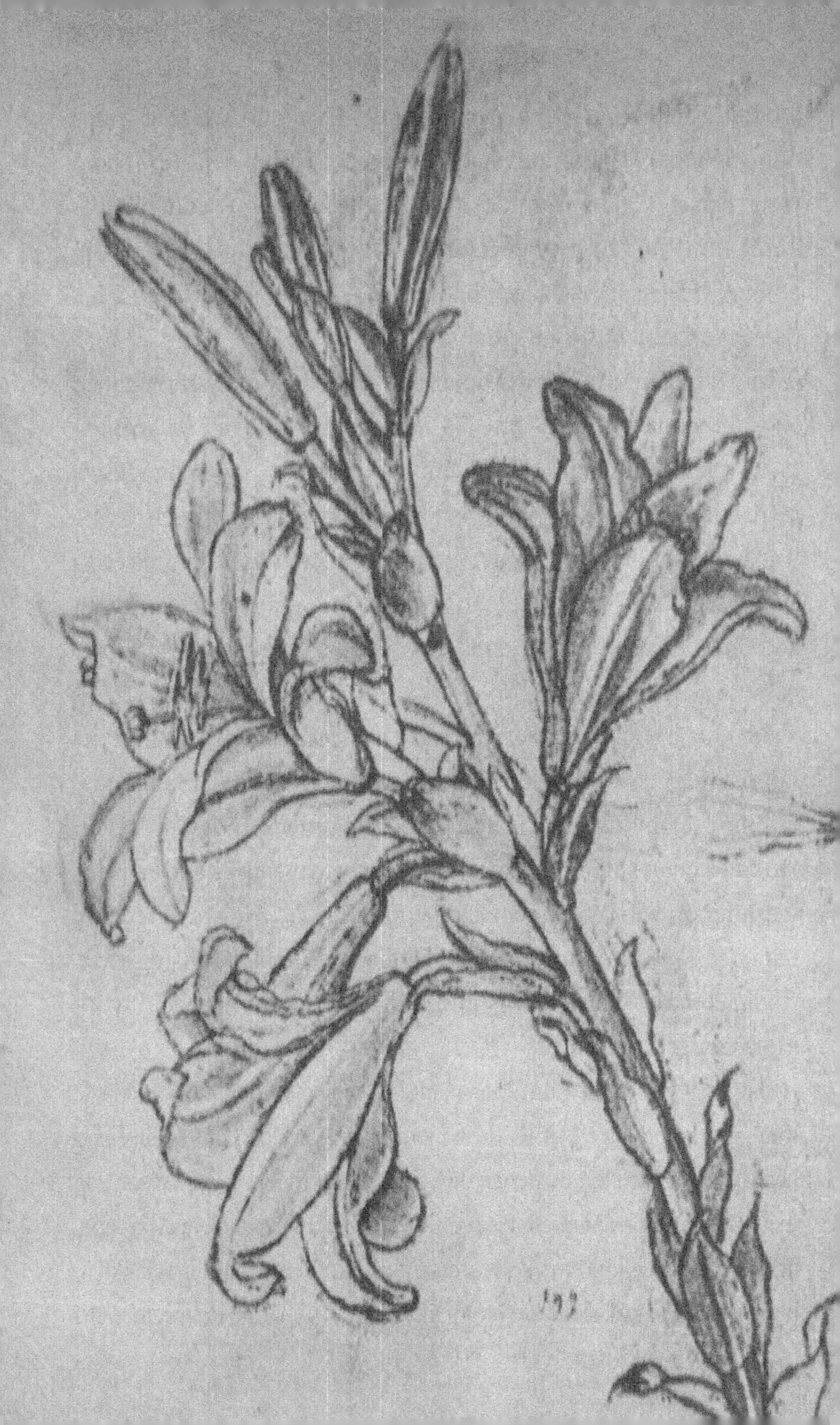

portraits are very life like and exhibit a sweet and sublime nature, they convey happiness and possess so much clarity and vivid sensuality, one could fall in love with them, however they do not embody the emotional depths and mystery that Leonardo's work does. Rafael was also an architect and was chosen to work on the Cathedral of Saint Peter after the death of Bramante. Some believe the reason for his untimely demise at 37 was because of exhaustion and a high fever.

There also lived another rising star, basking in his own light and working in Rome for the papacy, he was actually called "the sun amidst small stars" his name was Tiziano Vicelli also known as Titian. A disciple of the Bellini's and companion of Giorgione, Titian would take the art of painting to a whole new level. He was Venetian, like his friend Giorgione who was a more obscure and mysterious figure than Titian. He would have the great fortune of meeting Leonardo sometime around 1500.

Giorgione would go on to become a great but short lived genius who like Leonardo completed only a few but highly important works. His whole name was Giorgio Barbarelli da' Castelfranco, and was one of the most mysterious painters in the history of European art. A trait he may have acquired from his study of Leonardo, this is apparent in the uncertainty of meaning in most of all his work, but there is no denying his masterfulness.

Titian, a master in his own right and comrade to Giorgione painted in a very similar style with lightening speed and accuracy of execution. He would bring the art of color to a new dimension and portraiture to a new level of perfection not yet realized. It is very possible that he would cross the white light path of Leonardo while in Rome, and stand in awe of this universal master. Like his contemporaries, Titian was well aware of this man known as Leonardo the Florentine, the most valued artist in all of Italy, and the master that has set the bar for all the painters that would follow him.

Titian became a true genius of portrait painting. His work is superb in all its grace and perfection. His gifts are apparent and his understanding of refinement should no doubt be attributed to this master's master, Leonardo da' Vinci, who at this time soared above all the artists in Italy, yet found himself somewhat grounded by the inevitable and unstoppable new meteoric talents of the now highest period of the Italian Renaissance.

In Rome there was much change that ensued during the nearly twenty years he spent in the Lombard capital of Milan. The eternal city would foster the development of many great artists besides Michelangelo, Raphael and Titian; they were just three of the many shooting stars that entered the spotlight of the high Renaissance.

In the northern territories, from Florence to Milan and perhaps even Venice and beyond, Leonardo became adored and admired for his mastery and mind. He lived the life of a prince, yet more in demand than any prince could ever be. In Florence his home town, he became the heroic conqueror, born a bastard son of a bourgeois family who exceeded all expectations. Once a diamond in the rough and now the greatest ambassador of culture Italy has ever known. In Rome he subjected himself to a complex maze of new and aspiring talent and energy that must have taken him aback, and no doubt found it hard to keep up with. He was around 60 years old at this point in time and much of his own current occupations were kept in seclusion and his work not visible to many of the artists and patrons of Rome, however they were light years ahead of anything in the known world.

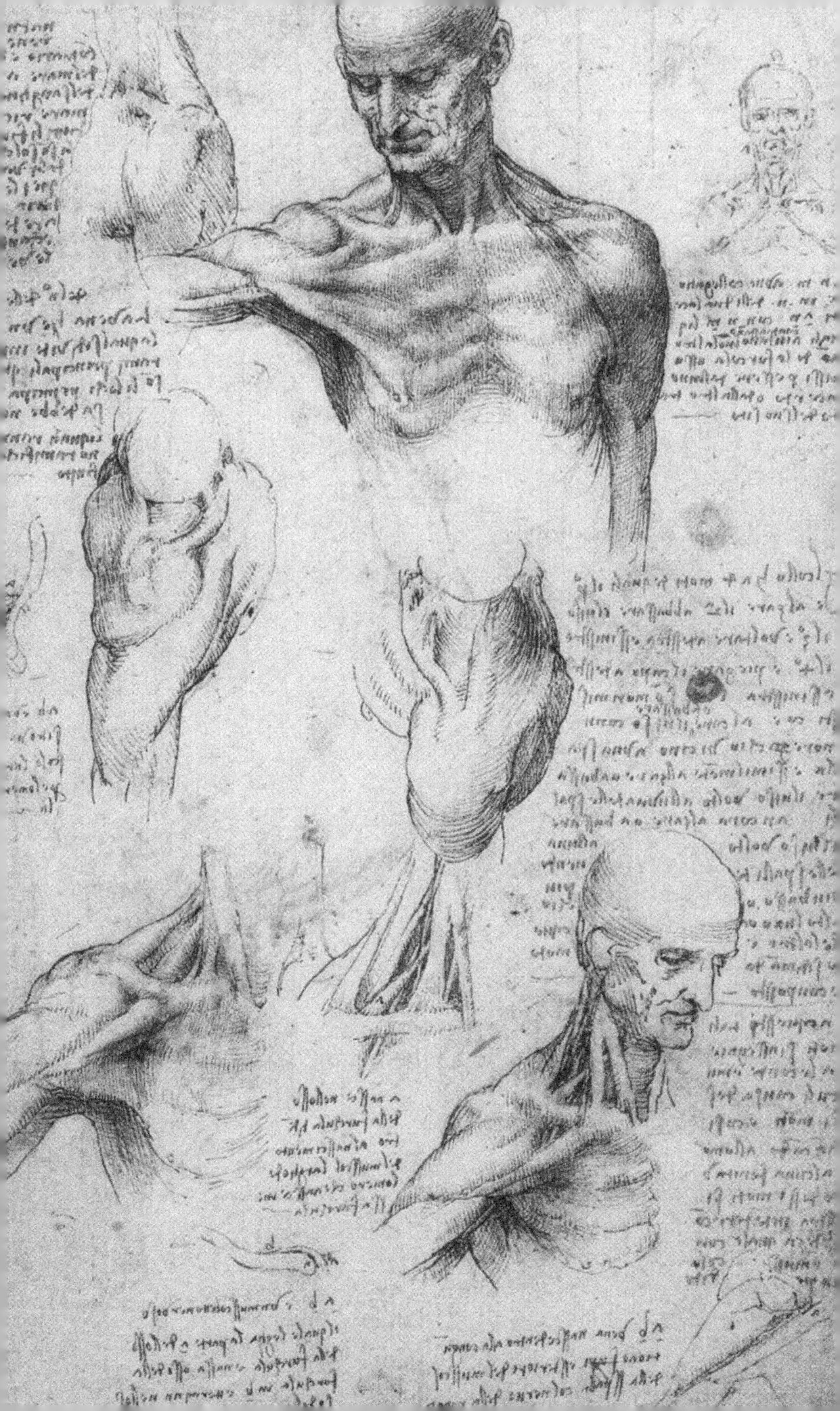

CHAPTER 10

HIS DEPARTURE FROM ROME AND HIS WORLD

IT WAS in 1513; Leonardo was near 61 years old and saw himself as a bit outdated and insignificant in the eyes of the Papacy and the Roman populous. He had no great achievements or even works to his name in Rome, only his reputation. Unlike his close friend Bramante he never thought the great city to be a priority like many of his contemporaries had thought, and now he would see that his avoidance had its consequences. His reputation, however, was well established and he was revered by all the artists and patrons in central and northern Italy, and he was treated with the utmost respect everywhere he went.

Leonardo, now under the protection of Pope Leo X, was living comfortably but forced into a solitary existence in the large rooms of the Belvedere far from the papal court. He began working on several projects and completed a book on the human voice. He was asked by Giuliano Medici to plan and execute the drainage of the Pontine marshes and redirect the Ufente river and create the drainage canal he called the Rio Martino. He also worked on parabolic mirrors to capture solar energy and enormous concave lenses for telescopic space observation, nearly one hundred years before Galileo. In addition to this work, he designed the machines to fabricate them, all of this during his time in Rome. There were also architectural projects to oversee for Lorenzo de' Piero Medici.

And for Leonardo, there were some difficulties he had to endure when he commenced his studies on anatomy and the skinning and dissection of corpses. He was asked to stop his work on the dissection of corpses by the papal court for it was still considered by many to be sacrilegious. This would not sit right with his need for scientific and anatomical research, and the fact that he was being overshadowed by the younger stars of Rome who were at this point beginning to eclipse his fame and being paid exorbitant amounts of money, would inevitably lead to his departure.

Leonardo would once again take to the road with his faithful entourage and his beloved little portrait of the *Mona Lisa* (Gherardini Gioconda). His destination this time would be Amboise, France where he received an invitation from none other than the king. He was given a beautiful place to rest his mind and reflect on everything he had done thus far. The king offered him and his assistants a very generous stipend.

His life at this point was more or less complete in many ways. Leonardo was around sixty five years old when his health began to fail. Prior to his departure from Rome there are some historians that believe Caterina, his biological mother, would become a member of his household sometime during these years but once again no one is absolutely sure of the facts. There are documents referring to a certain Caterina in regards to some funeral expenditures and one likes to think that Leonardo and his long lost mother were reunited but there exists very little proof of this ever happening. However it's nice to imagine that she decided to be with her brilliant and well to do son in her late years. It is very likely this Caterina was only a maid of Leonardo's household; the name itself was commonly used in Italy.

Soon his right arm became paralyzed and he could no longer paint. Francesco Melzi, Leonardo's most loyal and trustworthy pupil, would assiduously care for his master and ensure his peace of mind while assisting him in completing much of the studio work. His patron, King Charles of Amboise, would enjoy spending many hours in this illustrious master's presence, conveying his admiration for this universal being that graced his palace. They would discuss the many exploits and great achievements that occurred over his lifetime. The King would provide Leonardo with all and anything that was needed for his comfort and final resting place.

Leonardo was known throughout his life often to stop in the middle of his work to contemplate, becoming totally absorbed in soaring thoughts. But now he would stop to reflect on his distant past more often than not, his mind slowing in contemplation and much simpler discussions. He began to recall many of his shortcomings and the unfinished work he had left behind, not realizing how truly immense his legacy would prove to be and the magnitude of possibility his genius had created.

He would expound on his ideas and inventions that required more testing, his wings that needed more experimenting with, his experiments on optics and movement, astronomy and anatomy. He would modestly make reference to the over fourteen thousand manuscripts he created that had their significance and needed further exploration. The writing and research that would have been inevitably so important to mankind if only he had more time. He would remember with vivid description the great years in Milan when he became the Ducal courts most loved and admired Master, and reflect on his rich and exciting studies in

Pavia, the breakthroughs he made with his mathematical friend Luca Pacioli, and the early years in Florence with his beloved master Verocchio and the pupils and friends of his botega. He would recall all the learning and wonderful adventures during the Florentine years.

Leonardo would tell his King of his personal exploits as well, including his work with the many cadavers he dissected, the anatomical discoveries and advances he made. He would recall the troubles with the church, and some of the horrors he witnessed working for Cesare Borgia. The tragedy of his long lost great bronze horse which never came to be, the colossus Gran Cavallo, Sforza monument, he was commissioned to execute but never saw to its completion. His heartache clearly apparent to his king as he would ponder for a moment, perhaps stare at some random arbitrary shape on the Saint Cloix earth and feel his great mind in all its razor sharp imaginings, recapitulating in three dimensions the days, months, years, decades he wished to see again, but never would. With light speed his mind would race with a thousand images of nature and the secrets held within it that only he could divulge.

Leonardo da' Vinci would reach sixty seven years of age and then leave this beloved world for good. He died at Amboise, France on May 2, 1519.

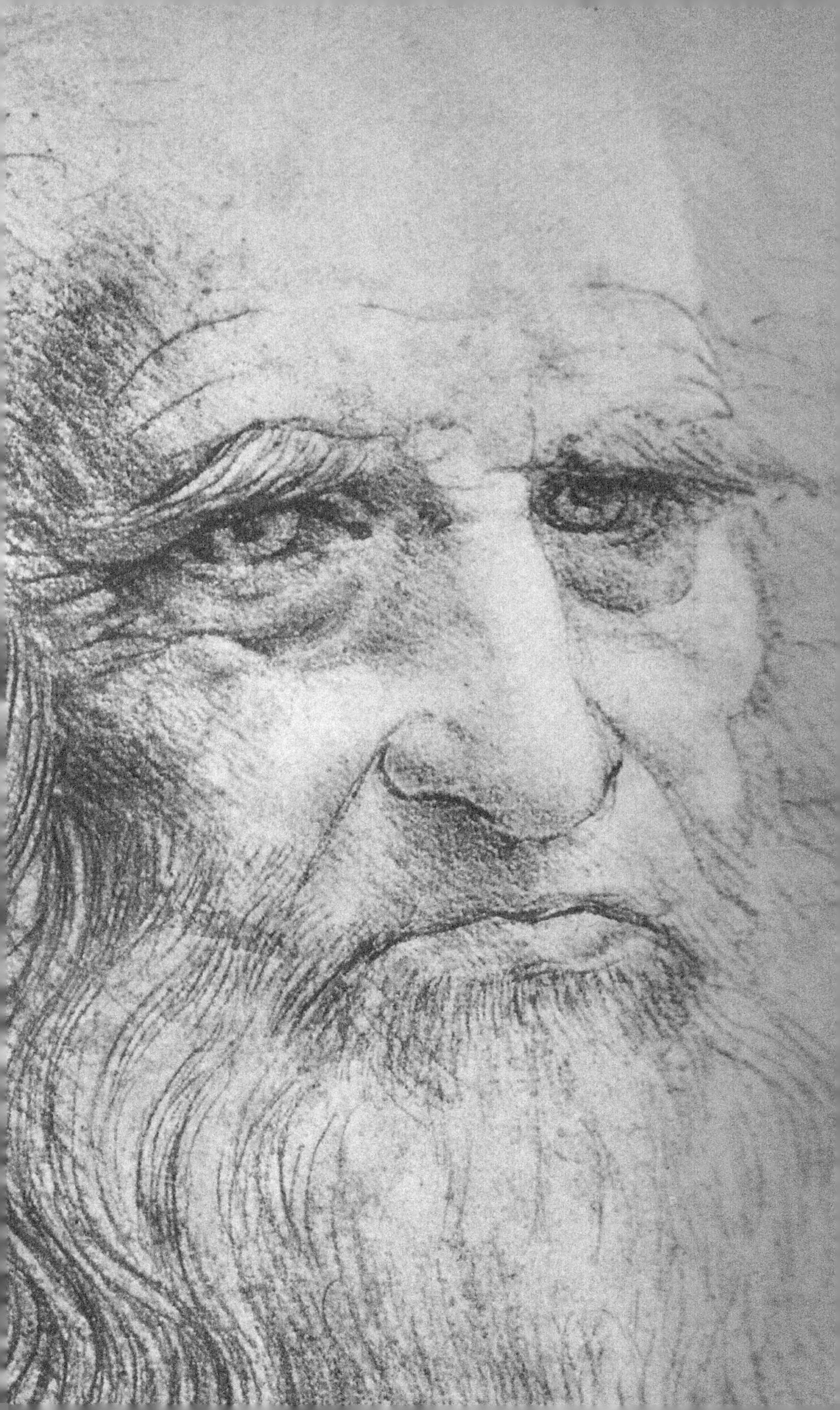

CHAPTER 11

HIS INFLUENCE AND EFFECT
–The most famous painting in the world

WHEN I am in the presence of a painting by Giotto or Massacio, I witness purity so apparent and so vital and real, yet at the same time witness something so very human and communicative through the artists spirit like nothing else. It's not the easiest thing to describe about a creative work yet it is one of the most important components of the work itself. This is the lasting and loving aspect I find in most all Italian Renaissance work.

The beautiful colors, expressions, and the thematic or narrative composition are the vehicles of communication; the style of the painter is his identification in which we distinguish the work. Leonardo da' Vinci's work shows this and in many cases much more than most of all these wonderful painters. Without emphasis on color or religiosity his work moves us into a realm of total fulfillment and abundant joy. They are emotional and complex yet evocative and engaging, they possess timelessness and perfection and they express true spirit and vitality.

Leonardo defines idealism like no other. This is why we remain transfixed by his work and in awe of his spirit. All of his work even the fragments that have survived, and everything he has brought into existence has the inherent qualities of a kind, spiritual soul. His adroitness and adeptness are apparent in all of his creations, whether a simple exercise in geometry or a more detailed sketch of a mechanism. His paintings and drawings and his sculpture and writings are only the beautiful remnants of his being. Leonardo was fortunate in that he did get to fulfill all his dreams.

He would say otherwise in his later years and recall his tendency to scatter his attentions. But now in retrospect, we as observers can actually see what one man is capable of achieving in one lifetime. His work will remain in essence a manifestation of his powerful spirit, alive and well in its fecundity and in its sublime conveyance of an ideal beauty. There are now in existence approximately 7,000 pages of precious manuscript representing nearly half of what was believed to be produced by Leonardo during his lifetime. The other 6 or 7 thousand manuscripts have vanished like so many of his fine sculptures and paintings. Much of Leonardo's work has been ravaged by time and abuse or vandalism and theft. Yet still he has left for us some astounding art that will always reveal the inspired qualities of his remarkable genius, his mastery of subtlety, blended hues and the magical truth of various details which give his sublime scenes such a living reality.

His drawings and the many pages of his thoughts so sweet with serene fluidity, masterfully blended tones, gracefully executed in his inimitable style so gently revealing in nature. They are works of a very perceptive mind and keenest of eyes, there is no mistaking his hand and his touch for perfection of form.

Leonardo's contribution to humanity appears even to this day so profound and vital that it's as if this extraordinary artist mind may have foreseen the spiritual needs, the aspirations and the technical achievements of modern times. His greatness was recognized

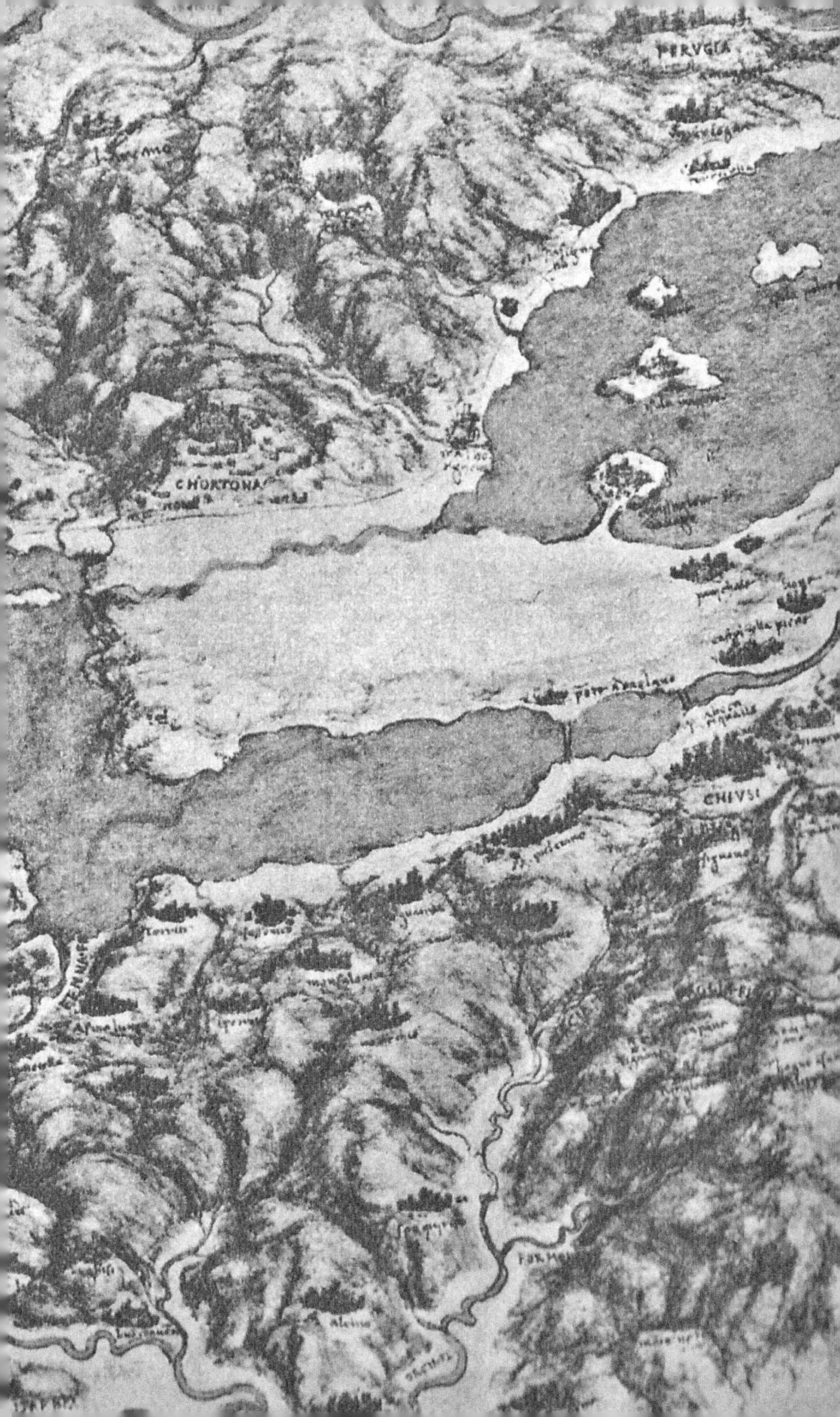

PERVGIA
CHORTONA
CHIVSI

while he lived, and without him the renaissance as a whole would have fallen short of these spiritual conquests that in turn brought light to all of European culture and then to the known world. All who knew Leonardo expressed their admiration for the talents, which God bestowed upon him. All of his teachings seem to throw light into all the dark corners of knowledge. There existed no other individual thinker with as much talent and drive in history as Leonardo da' Vinci.

There were many predecessors and contemporaries who displayed much genius and teaching but no one with such a diverse and prolific mind involved in so many varied pursuits could be compared to him. Even today nearly six hundred years later through study and close examination of him we have not exhausted the range of thought that he encompassed. Leonardo da' Vinci was and still remains the Universal Man of the ages.

To embrace him is to love him; to love him is to love life and everything in it that represents beauty and real meaning. Leonardo once said, "Art is the sole imitator of everything in nature." He expresses such a massive and diversified wealth of ideas, and conceptions that each mind that comes in contact with his rediscovers him differently. All of these minds however are convinced of the methodical exactness with which he pursued truth.

Leonardo's paintings are very moving, some would say disturbing and overall very mysterious in nature. To this day they are the most precious works of art in the entire world. They are also the most vandalized. People have attacked them with knives, stones, acid, and even fired shots at them, the Mona Lisa was stolen once, which is why it is now encased in bullet proof glass and guarded around the clock. It is safe to say that the portrait of Lisa Giaconda known as the *Mona Lisa* has been reproduced all over the world millions of times. Is it because of the portraits sublime beauty?

To me she stands for absolution and perfection, she represents the most supreme achievement of mankind. There is something so vital in her intrinsic qualities, and her image that is most reassuring. Her fame is mostly that of her master Leonardo, for no one really knows her, even historians are not sure of her true identity but we do know Leonardo painted her. This small portrait has changed the art of painting on many levels.

We love Leonardo and respect him for his kind and gentle disposition, his creative genius and mostly for what he has left behind, an appreciation for the highest of ideals and a universe of possibilities that he gave to us so generously along with the many tranquil intriguing moments to reflect on in our time, through subliminal means, which were created on a small and strangely shaped peninsula in the Mediterranean sea, once at the center of all the world in a place known as Italy during the fifteenth century.

~CHAPTER 12~
THE COURAGEOUS AND COMPLETE LEONARDO

THERE is no one in this life more courageous than an artist the likes of Leonardo da' Vinci. The heroics he has displayed are for most of us unfathomable. His will to create continuously and fearlessly was unstoppable. He was a true artist, who was dedicated to the creative life and the pursuit of the most important of human endeavors, the creative act, and with it, the production of infinite possibilities through raw talent and sheer expression of thought and feeling; through any and all creative means.

His life and work would in turn, take the earth and all of its inhabitants into a whole new realm and direction of endless and positive reformation. His legacy is unquestionably that of one of the most important and inspiring men in the pantheon of human achievement. To understand this we can begin to rejoice in his triumph, nourish in his spirit and carry on without any fear. We can express our love for life in which we dearly possess, and with this gift realize there is no end in knowing the fruit of this love or what it shall bare through creation, but one may witness its glory in the works of a creative soul the likes of Leonardo da' Vinci.

His paintings more than anything on this earth were and still remain divinely inspired and a direct injunction from heaven in which their meaning has become inscrutable and lasting infinitely. And in the presence of a masterpiece one must immediately acknowledge the existence of God and forego the existence of God even if only for a moment. And still there exists no glory on this beautiful earth more vital and lasting than the glory of nature and the sacred act of man representing that nature. Born to promote positive feelings and express the purist and most noble of all glorified ideals.

There are now millions of artists from all walks of life that find inspiration from other great masters of different periods and different parts of the world as well. This book is for those who thirst for some of that same inspiration through the great ones I have discovered.

EPILOGUE

Many of the ideas and innovations created during the renaissance maintain their significance and remain vital components to our present day life. Several of the great individuals I have mentioned in this book have contributed vastly to our world yet still remain obscure and unrecognized to most of us. The arts and sciences benefitted immensely through the multitudinous and courageous effort these extraordinary people provided.

Our language for example was born from this period in time; the Latin tongue was important to the learned and the academicians of the day. It would go on to serve as the root language of most Indo-European peoples. The Italian language developed into a brilliant and beautiful language and the science of philology was born.

Modern arithmetic and architecture were brought to new heights with advanced new approaches and new methods. Science and invention were becoming serious pursuits, and pioneering travel also important at this time, it was vital for trade and exploration.

Florence Italy was a melting pot for intellectuals. Along with its powerful banking families and thriving industries, it became the most culturally significant place on earth. There was little going on elsewhere in the world, perhaps Flanders and parts of Germany or Paris France, but nowhere else in the entire world was there a cultural phenomenon like that of the Italian Renaissance.

The rest of the planet was practically dormant in this regard. As was stated earlier about this unfeigned period of the most creative culture that expanded and changed our perceptions of this great world the early, middle and high Italian Renaissance that emerged out of the dark ages and brought us into the light as no other period in history.

UNIVERSAL MAN

Leonardo looks to the skies and realizes;
From here, his mind's eye can project an image of this earth turning silently poised on an axis of nothingness amid endless dark eternal space, moving immensely, perpetually, and perfect. From here he sees nothing wrong with this image, countless organisms electrify his imagination, colors illuminate ideas and present magnificent possibilities, shapes though beautiful are meaningless distractions, soft stillness's, pure creations, from here there is no real distance, no physical space, no time to distract or science to avoid, from here he embraces truth, boundless omnific heavenly truth, clear inexplicable and natural, from here he defincs love, assembles dreams and fashions hope, from here he discovers life, refines the soul and breathes universality.

From here he stands freely, and emboldened, proud, solemn, singular and fearless to create a world of promise and peace.

Richard Aliberti

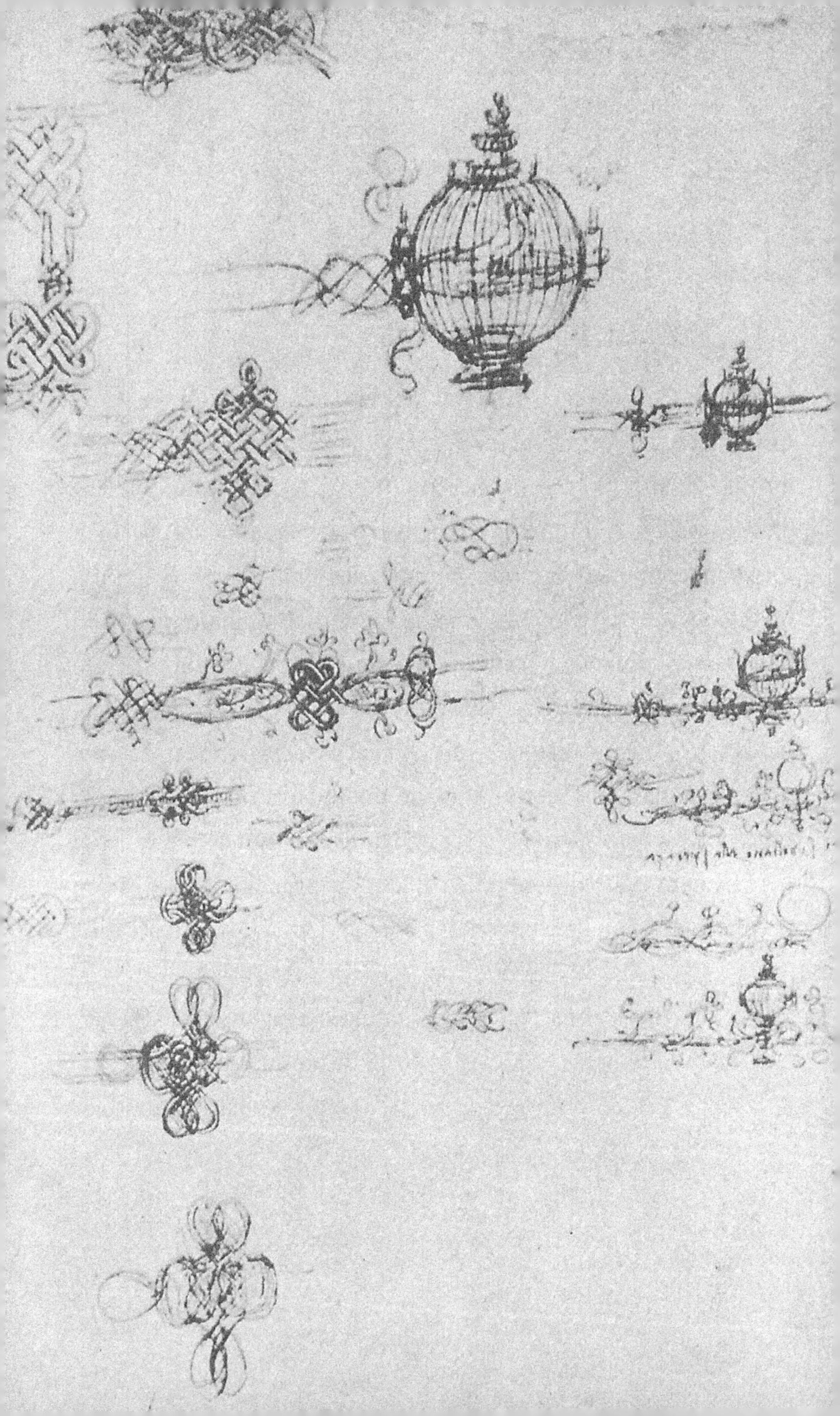

Index

Lippi, Fra Filippo 37
Lodovico 60
Lombard 94
Louis XII of Ligny 83
Lucia, Antonio and Mona 33
Lucia, Mona 33
Lucrezia, Borgia 84
lute 69

M

Machiavelli, Niccolo 62, 85
Magna Curia 12
Malatesta 70
manuscript 104
Masaccio 23
Masaccio, Tommaso 37
Masolino 53
math 83
mechanical drawing 75
Medici 49, 89
Medici, Cosimo 30, 54, 60
Medici, Giuliano 97
Medici, Il Magnifico 60
Medici, Lorenzo 30, 60, 69, 70
Medici, Lorenzo de' Piero 98
Melzi, Francesco 99
Michelangelo xiv, 63, 90
Micholozzo 53
Migliorotti, Atalante 69
Milan 77, 80, 94
Mirandola, Giovanni (Pico) 61
Mona Lisa 87, 98, 107

P

Pacioli, Luca 63
painter 70, 93
painting 91
palazzo Medici 54
parabolic mirror 97
Peace of Lodi 28
perspective 51
Perugino 69
Perugino, Pietro 43

ABOUT THE AUTHOR

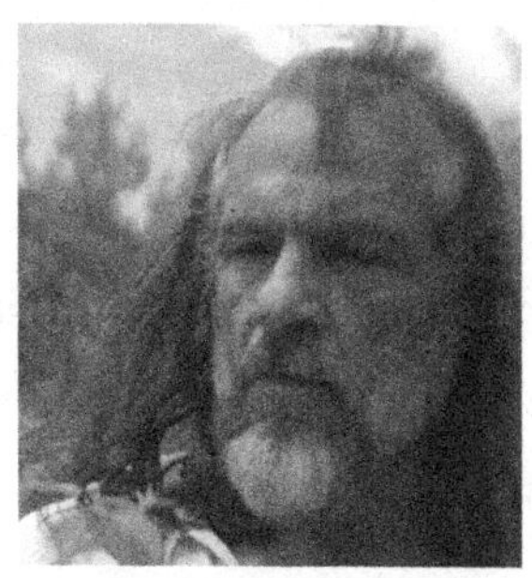

Richard Aliberti is an artist originally from Boston. The 3rd born son in a family of 7 children, Richard first became inspired by Leonardo da Vinci and the Italian Renaissance in his youth and throughout his early work he has nurtured that inspiration by building a career as a successful artist working primarily in the plastic arts through the media of painting and sculpture.

Some of his notable works include commissions of a bronze Dante Alighieri statue (that is at the Dante Alighieri society in Cambridge Ma) as well as commissions for several churches in and around Boston. Richard's work is also in a permanent museum collection in the Kennedy Museum on Cape Cod.

Most recently, Richard has been actively creating internationally, as he is embarking on some new chapters of his colorful and diverse professional experiences. This book is a part of that journey and readers of all ages and backgrounds will delight in the essence of the Italian Renaissance that awaits you in these pages.

SKETCH LIKE LEONARDO

In the blank spaces in the next pages, sketch and take notes on your observations of the natural world. Then upload your notes to the interactive Aliberti's Universal Man site filled with activities, videos, interactive tours of Italy, and more at www.leonardolives.com.

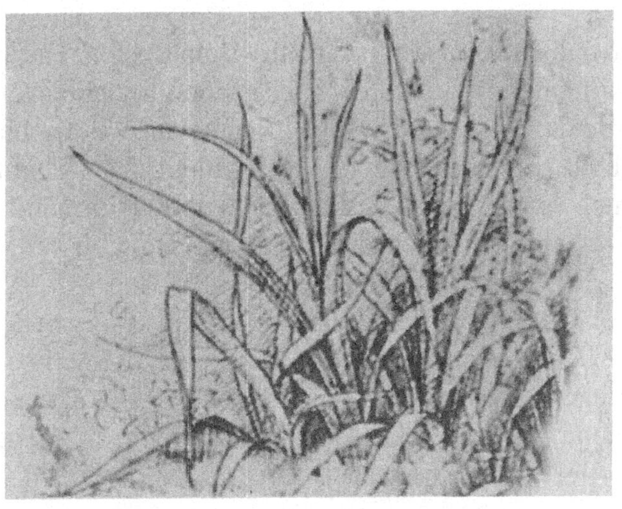

SKETCH LIKE LEONARDO

SKETCH LIKE LEONARDO

SKETCH LIKE LEONARDO

SKETCH LIKE LEONARDO

SKETCH LIKE LEONARDO

SKETCH LIKE LEONARDO

SKETCH LIKE LEONARDO

SKETCH LIKE LEONARDO

SKETCH LIKE LEONARDO

Made in the USA
Monee, IL
07 July 2026

56551159R00090